How to Help Your Three Legged Cat Be Happy & Healthy
Tripawd Basics
SECOND EDITION

Essentials of the Feline Amputation
Recovery and Care Handbook
from Tripawds

Includes Coupon for Premium E-book!

BY RENE AGREDANO AND JIM NELSON

HOW TO HELP YOUR THREE LEGGED CAT BE HAPPY & HEALTHY
SECOND EDITION: TRIPAWD BASICS
by Rene Agredano and Jim Nelson
A Tripawds Publication
https://tripawds.com

ISBN: 978-1-7334689-4-7

Published in the United States by:
Agreda Communications
240 Rainbow Dr., #14065
Livingston, TX 77399
https://agreda.com

Cover & Interior Design: Jim Nelson
https://about.me/jimnelson

Cover Illustration: Cat Vectors by Vecteezy
https://www.vecteezy.com/free-vector/cat

© 2006-2022 All Rights Reserved. TRIPAWD/s, the three-paw badge graphic, the slogan "It's better to hop on three legs than to limp on four", and "Be More Dog" are registered trademarks owned by Agreda Communications. All content herein is copyrighted and may not be distributed nor duplicated without express written permission.

DISCLAIMER: We (The Authors) are not veterinarians. All information provided herein is based only on our own experiences caring for our dogs Jerry and Wyatt, and the experiences of other Tripawds community members ring for amputee cats. This information is not a substitute for medical care by a qualified veterinary professional. Always seek the advice of a licensed veterinarian prior to making any medical decisions for your cat or undergoing any treatments or therapies, or if you have questions about your cat's health. We advise against any medical decisions made without the direct involvement of your veterinary team, and you should never delay treatment nor disregard medical advice based on something you read in this e-book or online at Tripawds.com. We do not guarantee that the information presented here will extend your dog's life, ensure a successful surgical procedure, or promote a complete recovery from amputation and cancer care. There is absolutely no assurance made of any outcome whatsoever. Neither safety nor efficacy is stated nor implied, directly or indirectly. Tripawds.com, is a project of Agreda Communications. René Agredano and Jim Nelson are not responsible or liable, directly or indirectly, for any form of damages whatsoever resulting from the use (or misuse) of information contained in or implied by the information available at Tripawds.com or within the pages of this document.

About this Book

Get More Help in Premium E-book.

This is the **Basics Versio**n of our premium Tripawds e-book, *How to Help Your Three Legged Cat*. To reduce the price, content has been removed and the formatting optimized for paperback printing. Recommended Reading lists and a detailed section about cannabis use for pets have also been truncated or removed.

For more comprehensive helpful information, photographs, active links, and bonus material, save **$5 OFF How to Help Your Thre Legged Cat Premium E-book** with Coupon Code: BASIC5

! Save now at:
https://tri.pet/tricatbook

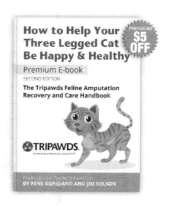

The true value of Tripawds e-books is the numerous direct links they contain to more helpful articles, videos, and podcast interviews.

NOTE: Underlined text throughout this book indicates active hyperlinks available in the premium e-book.

Dedication

This book would not have been possible without the coaching and cheerleading of Purrkins' mom, Holly. She has graciously given so much time and energy for the community and editorial help to make this book a reality, so tri-kitties everywhere can live better lives on three legs. Thank you Holly, we are furever grateful.

We are also deeply indebted to Fang's mom, Chantal. If she had not been the first brave feline parent to step into a completely canine community, tripawds.com would not be the helpful resource for all animals that it is today. Thank you Chantal, Fang's legacy lives on!

CONTENTS

About this Book	iii
You Are Not Alone	v
Introduction	1
You Are Not Alone	5
Deciding to Amputate	7
Why Cats Become Tripawds	19
Is Your Vet Qualified?	45
You Set the Tone for Surgery Recovery	55
Bringing Home Baby	73
Pain Management	81
Recovery	91
Helpful Gear for the Tripawd Cat	113
Rehabilitation and Continuing Care	123
Thank You!	147
Appendix	148
Bonus Materials	153
Acknowledgments	154
Tripawds Publications	155

You Are Not Alone

The Best Club Nobody Ever Wants To Join

Nobody ever expects their cat to lose a leg. If that happens, the Tripawds community makes the transition easier with education and emotional support. This handbook includes helpful tips for recovery and care. You will find **much more** help and support from many others who understand what you are going through in the Tripawds Blogs, popular Discussion Forums, Live Chat, and more at tripawds.com.

❗ For help finding the many Tripawds resources and assistance programs, start here:
https://tripawds.com/start

Connect with Tripawds:
- https://facebook.com/tripawds
- https://twitter.com/tripawds
- https://pinterest.com/tripawds
- https://instagram.com/tripawdscommunity
- https://linkedin.com/tripawds

It's better to hop on three
legs than to limp on four.®

INTRODUCTION

Don't just take our word for it...

Leading veterinarians and 15,000+ members recommend Tripawds community resources and support when coping with amputation recovery and care for three-legged dogs and cats.

Veterinary Industry Praise:

> *Tripawds is something you can check out, it's a community forum and you can learn and see that actually these dogs (and cats) do really, really well on three legs...*
> – DR. DEMIAN DRESSLER
> THE DOG CANCER VET

> *Tripawds...is a great community of three-legged pet owners... it's really a great resource where owners can share their experiences...*
> – DR. SUE CANCER VET
> WHAT TO KNOW ABOUT AMPUTATION

> *Tripawds has a very important role to play – to educate people about amputation, to discuss options, to help patients with amputations...*
> – DR. DENIS MARCELLIN-LITTLE
> UC DAVIS SCHOOL OF VETERINARY MEDICINE

> *If you and your pet are facing an amputation, or have just gone through one, you need to join Tripawds, the community website for three legged dogs and cats.*
> – MOLLY JACOBSON
> THE DOG CANCER BLOG

> *Tripawds is a place for people with three-legged pets – a community, a forum, advice about gear, nutrition... everything's there. I think it's phenomenal, a great resource that I send my [amputation] clients.*
> – MICHAEL "DR. T" TOKIWA
> THE COLLABORATIVE VET PODCAST

❗ Find more testimonials and podcast appearances with the authors on the Tripawds Media page. (https://tripawds.com/media)

From Tripawds Members:

> *Rene and Jim: First of all thank you for starting this much needed community. I do not know how I would of gotten through the last year without you.*
> – BROWNIE1201

> *"What a treasure trove of information and support you have created here! It's an excellent resource, I'm very glad to have found you all!*
> – RH3ANON

> *Thank you to everyone on this amazing site! It is so helpful to know that I have a place to go where people understand.*
> – KKILLIONMEULLER

> *The last 3 weeks have been a roller coaster and I couldn't have gotten through it without all of you.*
> – JO & HORACE

> *First of all, I absolutely love this site. It's helped tremendously with this new journey of continuing life with my pup as a Tripawd.*
> – ROMYTHETRIPAWD

> *I feel great comfort from reading all these messages, thank you for all the support. The more I read and the more videos I watch, the more settled I feel.*
> – KATHRYN84

Join the discussion at https://tripawds.com/forums

INTRODUCTION

Rene and Jim with Jerry, August 2008
https://bemoredog.net/about

Purrkins
https://purrkins.tripawds.com

Fang
https://cldavis.tripawds.com

Introduction

If amputation is a possibility for your cat, or you're thinking of adopting a "tri-kitty," thank you for downloading this guide. This book will save you time spent searching the Tripawds discussion forums and blogs. Inside you have all of the best health information the Tripawds feline family members have shared through the years – and then some! It's short but sweet, and we present this information to you so that your cat can stay as happy, healthy and fit as possible no matter what her age or current health situation. NOTE: For ease of reading, we refer to all cats as "she" or "her" in this book.

Welcome to The Tripawds Community

The Tripawds website launched in 2006 when our beloved dog Jerry was diagnosed with osteosarcoma, a painful bone cancer. Vets told us the best way to alleviate his pain was amputation, but we couldn't believe it. We wanted to help him, but we didn't know that an animal could be happy on three legs. How wrong we were! We went forward with the amputation and he amazed us for two beautiful years.

During that time, Jerry showed us that animals don't care how many legs they have. They don't look back and mourn their missing limb. They also don't think ahead and worry about the future. Jerry taught us that all animals live in the Now, and all they care about is having a happy home, good health and affection.

Our Feline Members Teach Us So Much!

Tripawds members have taught us lots through the years, and so do the many veterinary professionals we interview. Our goal has always been to provide the best amputation resources and support for pet parents. Nobody should ever have to feel as lonely and scared as we did when Jerry lost his leg.

Tripawds used to be all about the dogs. But over the years many feline parents have joined us. As a result, our knowledge about amputation for cats has grown exponentially. The first feline to join us was a brave kitty named Fang, and his mom Chantal. They started a tri-kitty blog while searching the web for a community to lean on during Fang's amputation and recovery. The more they shared their journey, the more they found that Tripawds has the best people around!

Fang's journey was so well documented that it didn't take long for other feline pet parents to discover it on the internet. Soon the Tripawds Nation had several three-legged cats in our community. Thanks to their generous information sharing and support, Tripawds.com now features the web's most extensive information about keeping feline amputees healthy and fit on three legs. This book is made possible thanks to each and every feline pet parent who has given their time, energy and love into making Tripawds the number one place for all animal amputees and their humans.

Help Your Tripawd Cat Be Happy. Here's What You'll Learn.

The information you're about to read is a compilation of Tripawds member experiences, veterinarian interviews, and community discussions at Tripawds.com. You will learn the most important things to know about keeping your cat happy on three legs, including:
- Why cats lose limbs
- How cats experience life as an amputee
- Understanding pain in cats
- Pre-amputation considerations
- Post-amputation recovery tips
- Differences between front and rear leg amputees
- The benefits of feline rehabilitation therapy and home exercise
- Nutrition and supplement tips
- And much more!

In between editions of this book, knowledge about feline health care grows as cats rise above second-class citizens of the vet world. New therapies for Tripawd cats are growing and information is always evolving. As we've done with our canine amputee handbooks, we will frequently publish new editions of this book. A free updated copy is available upon request to anyone who purchased the previous version within six months of the new release. Just send an email to jerry@tripawds.com with your order number.

We strive to present as much information possible, but if you have more cat-specific tips, recommendations and want to share your Tripawd cat's experience, please visit our Three-legged Cats Discussion Forum. Our community wouldn't be the comprehensive resource that it is without the contributions of members like you.

Please know that **we are not veterinarians.** We are only looking for ways to keep Tripawds healthy and strong. Generous veterinary professionals we interview make it possible to bring you the most up-to-date information about amputation recovery, and the needs of Tripawd cats. We promise you won't find unproven cures. And we do not advocate for one type of treatment or protocol over another.

Despite our efforts to remain current on the latest advances in feline health, veterinary science is constantly changing. What once held true yesterday might take a backseat to tomorrow's newer methods. We have made every effort to contact the most highly skilled and knowledgeable members of the veterinary and feline amputee community. However we can't guarantee that their recommendations will prevent injury or heal any existing injuries your cat might have already experienced. Please consult with your veterinary team about your cat's specific needs.

Our Promise: Guilt-Free Support

You'll see there are many ways to approach the amputation situation. We promise not to make you feel guilty over Tripawd care recommendations that you choose not to pursue. Everyone at Tripawds understands how amputation costs and follow up medical care can put a family in a financial hole. Take what you will from this information and do what you can, but don't beat yourself up if you can't implement all of these ideas. As a friend once told us, the best way to create positive change in your world is to do the least you can do...and then commit to doing at least that much.

When it comes to living life on three legs, there are no "right" or "wrong" choices, just well-educated ones. This book serves as an entry level guide to techniques that can help improve your Tripawd's overall quality of life. It's entirely up to you to take things one step further by working with your veterinarian to implement our suggestions.

May the life you share with your Tripawd kitty be healthy and hoppy for as long as possible!

Sincerely, Tripawds Founders Rene Agredano & Jim Nelson.

! Browse the Tripawds Blogs community and search the forums for the best feline amputation recovery and care tips or start your own free blog to share your story!

Quick Resources for Tri-kitties:

▶ Browse all Tripawds Cat Member Blogs
  https://tri.pet/trikitties
▶ Top Tips for Tri-kitties
  https://tri.pet/trikittytips
▶ Three Legged Cat Discussion Forum
  http://tripawds.com/forums/3-legged-cats/
▶ Tripawds Live Chat
  http://tripawds.com/chat
▶ Tripawds Toll-free Helpline
  http://tripawds.org/helpline

You Are Not Alone

Fear, loneliness and guilt are just some of many emotions that overwhelm us the minute our vet recommends amputation for a pet. Unless you've been through it before it's difficult to believe that amputee animals can be happy. But the reality is that animals usually do great on three legs. The truth is, only we humans carry the emotional burdens of limb amputation. We hope it comforts you to know that in our experience, out of all the animals who undergo limb amputation, cats usually do better than any other species! Sssh, don't tell the dogs this news!

After the vet drops the "A-bomb" it's hard to believe our pets can be happy on three legs. That's when the Tripawds Nation comes in to help. Our user-supported community's many free features, like the discussion forums, toll-free helpline, live chat room and blogs are available to anyone who needs information about amputating their pet's limb and living with an amputee animal. Here's a quick rundown of the best places to start your Tripawd journey:

The Tripawds Start Page provides an instruction guide to find what you need.

Watch our Tripawds Tutorial Video to learn how to navigate our community. You'll also learn how to connect with other tri-kitty families in our discussion forums (especially the Three Legged Cats Forum) and live chat room.

Finally, get detailed descriptions of other Tripawd cat experiences by browsing the more than 100 Tripawds Kitty Blogs.

Now, get cozy with your kitty and settle in for the education none of us ever wanted. When you're finished you'll be glad you learned about amputation and cats. No matter what you decide, at least you'll know you made an educated choice.

Need Help Navigating the Tripawds Community?

Tripawds is a network of more than 2000 three-legged dog and cat blogs. Members find the most help and support from others in the discussion forums. For information about our many resources and assistance programs, visit our <u>Start page</u>. Watch the <u>Tripawds Tutorial Video</u> for more help navigating our available resources.

Primary Tripawds Resources:

- Tripawds Community Start Page
  <u>https://tripawds.com/start</u>
- Discussion Forums
  <u>https://tripawds.com/forums</u>
- Tripawds News Blog
  <u>https://tripawds.com/progress</u>
- Tripawds Gear Shop
  <u>https://gear.tripawds.com</u>
- Tripawds Downloads Blog
  <u>https://downloads.tripawds.com</u>
- Nutrition Blog
  <u>https://nutrition.tripawds.com</u>
- Tripawds Gifts
  <u>https://gifts.tripawds.com</u>
- Tripawds Foundation
  <u>https://tripawds.org</u>
- Tripawd Talk Radio Podcast
  <u>https://tripawds.com/radio</u>

Connect with Tripawds on Social Media!

@Tripawds

- Facebook
- Twitter
- Pinterest
- LinkedIn

@TripawdsCommunity

- Instagram

CHAPTER 1
Deciding to Amputate

The Best Place for Help

Welcome to Tripawds, the community that nobody wants to join (but everyone is glad to have as a resource!). Try not to worry, you're in great company with people who understand what you are going through. Tripawds members are all concerned pet parents just like you. The most common reasons they join us are because of:
- Cancer
- Accidents
- Neglect / Abuse
- Congenital Limb Differences

This Decision is Between You and Your Cat

Most people consider three-legged pets as "handicapped." But once you meet a three legged cat, you will learn that they are anything but disabled! Meanwhile, learning about amputation is so overwhelming that it will send you running to family and friends for comfort. But before you share the news, be prepared for non-supportive feedback from some well-meaning but unenlightened humans.

If you are struggling with the amputation decision, the situation is often more difficult because of the emotional pressure a parent can feel from friends and family when they learn that amputation is being considered as an option. Most people believe that their cats are part of the family. But when it comes to hard costs, and the image of a "handicapped" cat, our friends and family will often surprise us with negative feedback.

Many people may draw the line of how far they will go for a cat when it comes to amputation and cancer care. They might say things like it's more humane to euthanize the cat than to "put her through that." Others may tell you that you're being selfish by wanting to amputate, or that you're crazy to spend so much money. All we can say is first, you have to forgive them. Then, turn around and ignore them.

Experienced Tripawd parents put it best when they say that money can be replaced, but your beloved kitty cannot. No matter what treatment you decide to pursue, always remember; this is a decision that is between you, your veterinarian and your cat. Ultimately only you know what is best for her.

Consider the Facts

Unless you have spent time with a Tripawd, it's hard to imagine that a cat will get around successfully on three legs. Here at Tripawds we like to say "Pets are born with three legs and a spare!" Not having that fourth leg can mean that your cat's balance and stamina may be challenged, but it doesn't mean they are handicapped. They just have different abilities and needs than a four-legged animal. When you feel uncertain about amputation, take a deep breath, and consider these facts:

FACT: Cats are experts at hiding pain.

Cats are masters at hiding pain. Most people don't think their animal is hurting because pets hide pain so well. Your cat probably isn't acting like she's in pain as far as you can tell. But if your vet is recommending amputation, the pain is severe enough to recommend removing the leg. Amputation recovery may appear to be horrendously painful. But even in the most challenging cases, pain experienced during recovery is nowhere near as bad as that from a fractured leg or growing cancer tumor. And it is manageable.

FACT: Your cat just wants to feel better.

Your cat doesn't understand if her leg is broken beyond repair. She doesn't even know what amputation means. What she does know is that she's in pain and wants to feel better. She wants to continue loving life, napping, playing and enjoying every minute without pain getting in the way. One thing we don't realize until our pet loses a leg is that animals do not feel regret, shame or anger about the situation. After the pain meds wear off, after a cat begins to regain her strength, she moves forward without looking back.

Amputation is not the easiest road to take. Some people would rather euthanize their cat than continue this journey. We never judge anyone for choosing that path. But we do want people to know that the majority of tri-kitty parents surveyed will tell you that amputation is a small price to pay for enjoying more pain-free, quality time together.

FACT: Animals live in the now.

Witnessing your cat's resiliency and extraordinary ability to get on with life is one of the greatest lessons that humans learn after going through amputation with their beloved friend. Those who have been through amputation usually see that their cat deals with it much better than people do.

When a cat loses a leg, the hardest part is getting the human to understand that post-surgery behavior like anxiety and nervousness is not usually depression or sadness. Oftentimes, it's just a cat's reaction to pain medications. Your vet can remedy the situation with some fine tuning.

! TIP: After surgery many pet parents second-guess the amputation decision when noticing their cat's change in behavior during recovery.

When this happens, don't panic. Felines deserve more credit than we give them. They are much more resilient than humans. Cats live in the moment, and have no regrets about losing a leg. Once a cat recovers, she will go on with life as usual.

For some cats battling cancer, their prognosis may only be a few months after amputation. Don't focus on that. The most important thing to remember is that it's quality of life that matters, not quantity.

If you're going to walk the amputation path together, follow your cat's lead and disregard the concept of "time." That's because animals don't frame their lives around calendars. They just live in the moment, enjoying each day with as much enthusiasm as the last. Animals show us the real meaning of "Living in the Now."

Is Amputation the Right Decision?

Amputation isn't for everyone and there is no one "right" decision. Only you know your cat better than anyone else. That knowledge will help you make the best decision for you both. When questioning amputation, ask yourself, "Is my cat strong/healthy/spirited enough to endure an operation like this?"

Nobody can guarantee that your cat will have a problem-free recovery and get along well on three legs after surgery. But most recover quickly and do great as Tripawds. Some factors, such as size, age and overall health can impact how your cat handles the change. But usually once the leg is removed and the healing begins, your cat will almost certainly begin to regain her old personality. Soon they start enjoying life again.

Of course every cat's situation is different, but we have seen the vast majority of our members' otherwise healthy cats adapt well to life on three legs.

Like any major surgery, there is a risk to being on the operating table. You can do things to minimize those risks. But if you proceed, you must prepare for the chance that something can go wrong. On rare occasions, it happens. There have been some cats who, for whatever reason either didn't make it through surgery or passed away a few days into recovery. Often it's because of situations that nobody could have predicted. But those incidents are rare. We see more success stories than tragedies in our community.

Amputation Gets Rid of Pain

As you struggle with this decision, keep in mind that amputation isn't getting rid of a leg; it's getting rid of the pain. Amputation alleviates the horrible pain a cat is experiencing.

If your cat is fighting cancer, amputation may or may not make it go away. Many cancers metastasize (spread to other parts of the body). But whether a cat is fighting cancer or undergoing amputation for another reason, it gives them a pain-free life, and more cherished memories.

Whether amputation allows your cat an extra month, year, or longer to lead an extraordinary life, that extra time is all about quality, not quantity. After amputation, every day together is icing on the cake.

We can't say if your cat is a candidate for life on three. But what we can tell you is we have seen cats of all ages, breeds and medical conditions adapt to life as a Tripawd. Some need more recovery time than others, and extra physical therapy might be needed. But the majority go on to live a normal, happy life.

In the Tripawds community, there are no right or wrong decisions about amputation. The only right decision is the one that's best for you and your kitty. Not every cat is a good candidate for amputation. Talk to your vet to find out if it's right for your cat.

What About Senior Cats?

What do you do if your geriatric cat is in a situation where a leg needs to be amputated? And is it cruel to even think about amputating on a very old cat? Those feelings are normal for any Tripawd but they are especially troubling when you love a senior pet.

For now, step back and try to be kind to yourself. No, you are not being selfish by considering amputation. As we like to say around here, amputation is not doing something *to* a pet, it's doing something *for* them. Once that bad leg is gone, the vast majority of animals continue living life as before. It's the humans that have a hard time with it!

> *She has gotten her spark back today. She went outside but then ran and fell. She is moving about quicker now...quicker than she has been in such a long time with that terrible sarcoma! This was the best decision to make.*
> - <u>SENIOR CAT PITTENS</u>
>   18 YEARS AND GOING STRONG ON THREE!

If you are hesitant about amputation because your cat is older or her prognosis is poor, remember, statistics are just numbers. While your vet can give you benchmarks and averages, your cat really is her own boss. A second opinion from another vet can ease your mind and confirm you're doing the best things pawsible for her. Remember, all pets are different. None of them will experience amputation and recovery quite the same way as yours will but in general, even senior cats do well with recovery and life on three.

Like life itself, there are no guarantees. Agreeing to the procedure is taking the leap of faith that everything will go as planned. It usually does! With luck and persistence at creating a tri-kitty-friendly environment your cat can bounce back successfully and have a chance at a great quality of life.

We hope to put your mind at ease with <u>these examples of elderly cat amputees</u> and their humans. Care to add yours? Please post in our <u>Three Legged Cats Discussion Forum</u> topic.

DECIDING TO AMPUTATE

> *Looking back to how worried and heartbroken I was when I learned we'd have to amputate, it absolutely was all worth it. I know she's an older cat, and despite the amputation I don't know how much longer I have with her, but from here on every moment I get with her is such a precious gift.*
> – HELPING A 15 YEAR OLD CAT RECOVER
>   @LEAUX

Amputation Costs and Related Concerns

Many of us spend more money on our pet's veterinary care than our own medical needs. Even so, the cost of care usually plays a big role in what we can or can't do for our animal companions. None of us like to put a dollar amount on our pets, but the fact is that most of us do not have unlimited resources to pay for care. There's nothing wrong with thinking about veterinary care costs, but choosing the vet with the lowest price doesn't guarantee the best medicine either.

If you received an amputation surgery quote that seems extraordinarily high, keep in mind that amputation costs can vary depending on several factors including:

- **The vet who is doing the surgery.** Specialty clinics and their surgeons cost more because they have more experience, newer equipment and more staff to care for patients.
- **The complexity of the amputation itself.** Cancer usually presents more complex circumstances for amputation surgery.
- **And finally, the cost of care where you live.** Vet care prices vary from region to region, and country to country.

> **! TIP: Comparing Surgery Estimates**
> When comparing amputation and treatment estimates, always compare apples to apples. Make sure the clinics you are considering are quoting you on the exact same care services.

One of the most popular questions we hear at Tripawds is, "Should I use a specialty vet or have my family vet do the amputation?" It's a fair question. We know that many family vets can do amputations just as well as a board-certified surgeon. But many family vets don't do more than one or two amputations a year. So if you have the ability to pay for a specialist who does them all the time, you increase the odds that if any problems occur, your cat will be in very experienced hands.

Amputation is a major operation and complications can occur. Specialty clinics are equipped with the newest equipment that minimize risks. Their teams are highly skilled at handling challenging cases. Veterinary care expert <u>Dr. Nancy Kay</u> advises us to...

> *Keep in mind the potential for complications. If a significant complication occurs due to substandard care, you will end up spending a great deal more money treating it, not to mention associated emotional energy, than you would have spent at the better more expensive clinic to begin with.*
> – DR. NANCY KAY

What Does Amputation Cost?

Never feel guilty about factoring money into your decision. Veterinary care is more expensive than ever. Few of us have unlimited resources, and must consider prices when deciding. Here is a Tripawds discussion forum topic that can give you a better idea of feline amputation costs (mostly from our North American members):

▶ <u>Costs of Amputation and Chemotherapy for Cats: What Did You Pay?</u>

As of 2022, the average amputation costs for cats is anywhere from $2,000 to $5,000 USD. Overall costs will vary depending on whether or not you are amputating because of cancer, which requires additional diagnostics for the overall procedures.

! TIP: If You Need Financial Help

In the U.S., as of 2020 only about 17 percent of pet insurance policies are for cats. Unexpected veterinary bills can devastate our finances. It's tragic when humans can't cover the costs of amputation for their beloved pets. Some are able to get help, but many others are forced to euthanize their cat because they can't afford surgery. If you are caught in the heartbreaking situation of not being able to pay for your cat's care, please don't give up. There are organizations that might be able to help, including the Tripawds Foundation [Amputation Surgery Assistance Program](#).

Is Your Cat an Amputation Candidate?

Even the best vets and well-informed pet parents sometimes have misconceptions about which cats are good candidates for amputation. Many people, even some vets, will look at an older cat and dismiss them as a candidate. The same goes for cats with arthritis or those who have had previous limb surgeries. Those cats might also be seen as bad candidates. But deciding whether or not a cat can do well on three legs requires a holistic look at the entire cat, not just one aspect of their health history.

Consider your cat's entire health picture.

Your cat's overall health history and personality are the biggest factors that determine how well she can do on three legs. The healthier the cat, the better the outcome no matter their age. Some vets dismiss a cat as an amputation candidate because the cat has arthritis or another chronic condition like diabetes. That's easy to do when a vet hasn't seen too many feline amputees in practice and have limited experience on which to draw from.

We are not vets ourselves, but orthopedic veterinarians have told us that age and size alone should not rule out any animal for amputation surgery. The animal's whole health picture needs to be assessed before deciding. In our community we have seen many members' cats with existing conditions have good recoveries and happy lives as Tripawds.

Are you ready for your cat's post-op care?

Consider the logistics of caring for your cat during recovery. For example, who will provide care for your cat after surgery? Can you stay home for a few days to manage recovery? It usually takes about two weeks of regular monitoring to make sure your cat is healing properly. Amputation recovery is like bringing a baby home from the hospital. If you can't give that amount of time to recuperation because of work and family obligations, do you have a support system in place? Can anyone help you?

Is Your Cat Overweight?

Overweight cats have a big challenge when it comes to getting along on three legs. But losing weight isn't impossible. If you're dedicated to helping your cat lose weight after surgery, once the pounds come off they can enjoy an excellent quality of life. Tripawds need to use their body differently than other cats, so it's critical that cats stay slender, almost underweight, in order to reduce the joint stress. You must be vigilant about managing food intake to make mobility easier.

The veterinary pain management guru, Dr. Robin Downing of Windsor, Colorado, once told us that a Tripawd should be about a 3.5 to a 4.0 on the canine and feline body condition scale. Overweight cats can make it through surgery and recovery if their humans work hard at dropping the pounds. We will always help you get there in the Tripawds Eating Healthy Discussion Forum and archived posts in the Tripawds Nutrition blog.

How's your attitude about life on three legs?

Some people don't want to amputate because they believe that living with one less leg is cruel or unnatural. What many forget is that animals don't have an issue with being an amputee, it's the humans who have a harder time with the idea.

However you experience it, we can almost guarantee that your experience will be different from other Tripawds in some ways, and very much alike in other ways.

Worried about your cat's quality of life after surgery?

Our community conducted a 2020 Quality of Life survey for cats and dogs. The questions are based on the very first *Amputee Pets Quality of Life Survey* published by Dutch researchers in 1999. Here's what feline Tripawds members had to say about how their cat adapted to amputation. When our members were asked if they would choose amputation again, the overwhelming response looked like this:

> *Yes I would, because I was amazed at how quickly he adapted to life as a tripawd and how well he recovered. I was scared at first and my spouse and I thought we would be sad every time we looked at him, but its actually the opposite. My cat is still full of energy, jumps, runs (very fast!) and plays as if*

he never had surgery. I also did some research before making a decision on whether or not to amputate (or having the surgery to try and fix the broken bones, where the recovery time was extremely long and might have been painful/risk of infection, etc.) I don't regret my decision at all.

Other organizations' amputee quality of life surveys reflect the same findings. Check out the non-profit <u>International Cat Care organization survey about cat amputation</u>.

ICC survey results revealed that out of 230 amputee cats, over 90% of owners believed that their cats had a normal quality of life after the amputation. Most owners were very confident that amputation did not significantly impact on their cat's quality of life. When asked whether they would make the same decision if they knew then what they knew now, 95% of owners said, "Yes!"

Does Your Cat Act Her Age?

Some people think that as cats near the end of their projected life span, amputation recovery will rob them of any precious time left. The risk is real, but we must remember that no matter what the age of the cat, the pain associated with their condition requiring amputation is likely worse than the pain of recovery itself. And even if a cat's prognosis is short, amputation enables them to experience less pain during their remaining months.

If age is holding you back from amputation – and your vet believes your cat is a good candidate – hopefully this reassures you that even an older feline can recuperate without problems.

Is a Prosthesis in Your Cat's Future?

Despite their remarkable ability to bounce back after losing a leg, all Tripawds have a greater potential for developing chronic aches, pains and injuries than their four-legged counterparts. An artificial limb can decrease those problems, but using one takes dedication, time and money.

Artificial limbs for amputee pets have come a long way in the last few years. New pet prosthetic designs show up in the media all the time. Despite these advances, important questions about pet prosthetics are still unanswered, especially when it comes to cats. For example, there is still no concrete data about:

▶ To which level can surgeons amputate a leg and

successfully attach a prosthetic?
- What amount of time and rehab therapy is required for adapting to a device?
- How do younger animals adapt to prosthetics when compared to older ones?
- What kinds of breeds and body types are more successful at adapting to prosthetics?

"This is not a simple task and a huge learning curve for veterinary medicine," says Dr. Felix Duerr, DMV ACVS Diplomate, ACVSMR, who oversees the Small Animal Sports Medicine and Rehabilitation program at Colorado State University Veterinary Teaching Hospital.

Despite the many unknowns, some cats are currently enjoying a better quality of life with prosthetic devices. If you're interested in a prosthetic, it starts with proper evaluation by an orthopedic surgeon. You'll need a team consisting of a veterinarian, a certified rehabilitation therapist, a veterinary prosthetician, and YOU.

If you're willing to make a long-term commitment to rehabilitation therapy, a device from a qualified pet prosthesis designer like OrthoPets can improve your Tripawd's quality of life. A prosthetic takes stress off the remaining limbs. It also decreases the chances of long-term injuries caused by the modified stance and gait that all Tripawds develop over time.

! TIP: Prosthetic limbs must be considered **before** amputation surgery.

If you are considering a prosthetic for your cat, it is critical to let your veterinary surgeon know prior to amputation. The best candidate for a prosthetic is a cat who will have at least three-quarters of the entire limb left intact after the amputation. That's roughly just above the wrist or ankle joint. This gives the prosthetic something it can grab and connect with the body.

Your veterinary surgeon should also have a good working relationship with a reputable pet prosthesis designer like OrthoPets. If not, and you want to investigate cat prosthetics, you need to find a vet who is comfortable supporting you in the decision.

You Know Your Cat Better Than Anyone Else

All cats are different, just like people. What's right for one may not be right for another. If your intuition says that your cat could be a good candidate for amputation surgery, but your vet is not on board, we encourage you to seek another opinion.

Some vets who aren't as familiar with the extraordinary lives of Tripawds may quickly dismiss a cat as a candidate because of her age, or size. If your vet does this, please consider getting a second or even third opinion. Another perspective can mean the difference between a hasty farewell or a few more months or years of pain-free living.

Recommended Reading:
▶ Extensive reading lists with links to related articles and videos are available in the Premium E-book. **Save $5 OFF with coupon code: BASIC5**
https://tri.pet/tricatbook

CHAPTER 2
Why Cats Become Tripawds

Common Reasons for Feline Amputation

Nobody ever expects their four-legged family member to lose a limb. When it happens to you, it seems like you're the only one out there facing the big amputation decision. But we promise, you're not. Check out these common reasons why many cats become Tripawds.

Accidents

Similar to Tripawds dog members, the vast majority of felines join our community because of cancer. However if your cat is losing a limb for another reason, you're not alone. Accidents make up the second most common reasons why felines lose limbs.

<u>Car accidents like Becca's</u> are common. One of the most unusual accidents reported was when <u>Misu, an eight month old Tortoise kitten</u>, got a rear leg stuck in the box springs of her human's bed!

> *Upon further inspection it was evident that Misu had gotten inside the box spring and had gotten her back leg trapped in a spring... It was evident her foot was badly broken, but there was no easy way I could free her without risking severe injury to myself from her extreme distress. Luckily I remembered a jeweler's saw in my tool box and ran to get it. I began sawing through the springs and by the time I was almost through the second one, she managed to pull free ...*
>
> – <u>READ MORE ABOUT MISU</u>

Many other Tripawd kitties prove that life on three legs can be great, even after a terrible tragedy. For example:

- <u>Stevie</u> lost his leg to a pit viper snake!
- <u>Marmalade</u> came to a shelter with a non-functioning leg.
- <u>Honey</u> was found in a driveway with a de-gloved leg after getting caught in a car engine.

- Ian Fluffypaws had an unfortunate encounter with farm equipment.
- Smore suffered a gunshot to her leg as a kitten.
- Bobby, was a giant kitty who got tangled in a bear trap.
- Tumbles, endured three surgeries in three months as a kitten at 6.5 months old after an unknown type of accident.

These are just a few of the many different stories of amputations resulting from different types of accidents found in **all Tripawds cat blogs**.

Limb Differences and Congenital Issues

Second to accidents, many feline members lost their limb for reasons like infections and congenital abnormalities. If a malformed limb creates mobility problems, the veterinarian often suggests amputation. These cats are some of the most fortunate Tripawds. If most of the malformed limb can be saved, that cat could be a perfect candidate for a prosthesis.

Usually most cat parents don't go the prosthesis route, probably because cats are tougher to train to use them. Most skip the artificial limb, just because cats are even more agile on three legs than dogs. Some examples of cats with limb disabilities who later became three legged include:

- Feta the Three-Legged Wonder Cat who lost her leg to infection.
- Steve the Pretty Tripawd Kitty who was born with malformed tendons and ligaments.
- Twister who was born with malformed rear legs

And then there's **Anne Bonny, The Swimmer Kitty**. This girl was born with "Swimmer Syndrome," a rare condition in newborn kittens which creates weak legs that splay outward. One of Anne's rear leg had problems too, so amputation was the recommended way for her to live a happy, normal life.

Cancers of the Limb

Cancer is still the primary reason most cats become amputees in the Tripawds community. When a cat (or any pet) is diagnosed with a limb cancer, vets typically give pet parents the option to:
- amputate only,
- amputate and follow up with radiation and/or chemotherapy,

▶ skip surgery and go straight to palliative care for pain relief via medications and physical therapy modalities like acupuncture, until quality of life diminishes.

The prognosis for many limb cancers in dogs is poor, but cats often fare much better. For example, many limb cancers come with a prognosis of less than a year for dogs, but not cats. A good example is the aggressive cancer known as osteosarcoma (OSA). Although it doesn't develop as rapidly in cats, a retrospective feline osteosarcoma study shows the risk of metastasis exists. The good news is that most osteosarcoma cats go on to live out their normal life expectancy unless other serious medical conditions develop.

Sometimes a feline member has a serious form of cancer with a grim prognosis. When that happens, amputation surgery and recovery might not seem worthwhile. But again, consider that amputation gets rid of pain. Doing so can provide a better quality of life, or whatever time the cat has left. But if there's one thing we've learned since we started Tripawds in 2006, it's that cancer prognoses are just educated guesses based on averages. They do not address what is going on with your cat's unique physiology. And as bad as a prognosis sounds, even the smartest vets cannot precisely predict how cancer will behave. In our community we've seen many animals with serious forms of cancer live far beyond their prognosis.

Little Man the Tripawd Cat was the perfect example. He was given a prognosis of just nine months to live when vets discovered he had a Feline Injection Site Sarcoma (formerly referred to as a "Vaccine Associated Sarcoma"). Four years later Little Man celebrated his 13th birthday. He's an angel now, but we can still learn much about living with cancer through his long, happy life as a Tripawd.

If your cat is facing a serious cancer, remember that she doesn't care if she is given a week or a month or a year for a prognosis. As much as cats want you to think they can count, they really don't mark days off calendars or know when their time will be up. And even if they could count, a year to a cat is a long time when considering their already extremely limited lifespan.

For now, let's take a look at different cancers that affect cats and cause them to lose limbs.

Osteosarcoma

Osteosarcoma (OSA) is a malignant (capable of spreading) limb cancer. It's the most common one diagnosed in dogs, but osteosarcoma in cats is relatively rare. Regardless, Tripawds has been around long enough to encounter at least a half dozen members who joined because of the disease.

Nicholas is one of many cats with osteosarcoma who have joined us through the years.

> *One unfortunate side effect of this is misinformation. A lot of people don't realize that osteosarcoma carries a radically different prognosis in the cat, because it doesn't typically metastasize. VCA's feline osteosarcoma site (my first hit when I Google "osteosarcoma in cats") gives canine statistics and treatment recommendations that don't apply to cats.*
>
> – NICHOLASANDCOMPANY

Osteosarcoma tumors appear in humans, dogs and cats. This painful condition occurs when bone cells go haywire and replicate into a tumor mass that starts destroying bone material in one location. Generally it appears in a limb. On rare occasions can form in other bones such as the skull or ribs. This cancer will almost always spread to the lungs ("metastasize") in dogs. Vets used to think it didn't spread as quickly in cats, but new research shows that bone cancer likely metastasizes in cats more often than previously believed.

Clinical signs of osteosarcoma usually begin with an occasional limp. Sometimes there is a hard swelling where the tumor is growing on the affected limb. The area may be painful to the touch. Bone cancer tumors weaken bones so if a cat has osteosarcoma, there is always the possibility that the bone might shatter on impact with a hard surface, or turning the wrong way. This is known as a "pathologic fracture." These breaks do not heal or stabilize.

Osteosarcoma in cats can go undetected for an extended period of time.

If all other potential conditions are ruled out, it makes sense to look for it. To reach a diagnosis, your vet will conduct a full exam of your cat. Radiographs (x-rays) will be taken in two places: 1) the affected limb and 2) the lungs, to find out if the cancer has spread to the lungs.

If the cancer has spread, life expectancy is considerably shorter. Vets usually recommend palliative (pain management) care instead of amputation, until the cat is no longer able to remain comfortable. And if it has not spread, chemotherapy may be a good choice to prevent metastasis later on. Usually an x-ray is enough to diagnose bone cancer.

Is Chemotherapy Required?

If it is determined that a cat has osteosarcoma, amputation will get rid of the pain from the bone tumor. Because it is such a slow growing type of cancer, vets historically believed that chemotherapy is optional. The Society of Surgical Oncology states that "amputation alone without chemotherapy may be curative in cats with appendicular OSA." However, this new study in 2022 may change that perspective. New science appears to be leaning toward amputation and chemotherapy as the recommended treatment for cats who lose a leg to this cancer.

Some Tripawds members who have cats with osteosarcoma decided to undergo chemotherapy as a precaution. Jill the Cancer Fighting Tripawd Kitty is one member who did. Her blog is a great read if you are facing osteosarcoma.

> *It's been three years since Jilly was at the hospital having her leg amputated. Three years since her journey began. Now here we are. She's a happy, healthy kitty. Looking at her you would never know she was ever "sick". You would never ever know she had cancer, went through a major surgery, went through chemotherapy, went through chemo, tried another treatment that made her so sick she lost 25% of her body weight. She is as happy and healthy as she's ever been in her entire life.*
> – JILL'S JOURNEY

Chondrosarcoma

This limb cancer is even rarer in cats than osteosarcoma. Chondrosarcoma in cats is a cancer that appears in cartilage, the connective tissue between bones and joints. Scientifically described, chondrosarcoma is comprised of "firm, rapidly growing masses attached to the underlying bone; they cause lameness and are painful on palpation. Grossly and histologically, the tumor is similar to that described in the dog. Metastasis to the lungs has been found in 10% of the cases," states this "Primary and Secondary Bone Tumors in the Cat" paper. Published by the University of Pennsylvania Veterinary School, the paper explains how this cancer grows rapidly and if it's not caught and treated early enough it can be life-threatening. Oftentimes it can metastasize to the ribs or other parts of the body.

The majority of feline chondrosarcoma tumors appear in the flat bones and often result in a leg fracture if not diagnosed early enough. Once diagnosed, your vet will usually recommend amputation and sometimes chemotherapy. However, chemotherapy for chondrosarcoma hasn't been fully studied for its effectiveness in treating the condition. This is a rare cancer in cats but just like osteosarcoma, there are the exceptional few who have lost legs to this rare condition.

Tripawds members with chondrosarcoma include:
- Fang, diagnosed at 11 years old
- Charlie, diagnosed at 10.5 years
- Sebastian, diagnosed at an unknown age.

> *It's been a busy six months since Charlie had his surgery, so I wanted to come by and give an update! The bottom line is, Charlie is doing great! His pathology finally came back and I am happy to say that it was confirmed that he did have a chondrosarcoma and that the margins were clean. He should be able to live out his natural lifespan and it is very unlikely that the cancer will recur. Great news!*
>
> – CHARLIE THE CAT

Jerry Cat also had chondrosarcoma, diagnosed at age 14.

> *My cat was originally thought to have osteosarcoma, but tests came back with the diagnosis of chondrosarcoma and he needed his scapula and right front leg amputated. He lived happily and healthily for almost 2 and a half years after the amp, and succumbed to suspected lymphoma over a weekend in Oct. of 2017.*
>
> – BOXERHATTIE

Soft Tissue Sarcomas

Soft tissues sarcomas (STS) are common in the Tripawds feline community. This type of cancerous tumor originates in the body's non-bone connective tissues and accounts for about seven percent of all feline skin and subcutaneous (lowermost layer of the skin) tumors. The term "soft tissue sarcoma" is a blanket term used to describe several types of locally invasive connective tissue cancers that behave similarly. These cancers include:

- fibrosarcoma
- hemangiopericytoma
- liposarcoma
- rhabdomyosarcoma
- leiomyosarcoma
- malignant fibrous
- histiocytoma
- malignant nerve sheath tumors (neurofibrosarcoma, schwannoma)
- myxosarcoma
- myxofibrosarcoma
- mesenchymoma
- spindle cell tumor

All of the above tumors behave similarly in the body. Researchers say they almost always:

- Originate anywhere in the body
- Appear as an easily removed, single "encapsulated" tumor when in reality it has long "tentacles" that reach deep within skin layers and make complete removal extremely difficult.
- Frequently return, especially if the surgeon did not completely remove the tumor.
- Metastasize (spread) through hematogenous (blood) routes
- Have a poor response to chemotherapy and radiation therapy for high-grade tumors
- And all share a low to moderate metastatic rate

Feline Injection Site Sarcoma – FISS
(Formerly referred to as "Vaccine Associated Sarcoma")

Many cats develop a lump at a vaccine site and in most cases the lumps resolve on their own within a few weeks. But starting in the early 1990s veterinary scientists discovered a correlation between certain types of feline vaccines and cancerous tumors, naming them "Vaccine-Associated Sarcomas." The correlation between STS tumors and certain types of vaccines given to cats is widely accepted by veterinary researchers and today most scientists refer to them as "Injection Site Sarcomas."

If your veterinarian is confident your cat is affected by the condition, Tripawds member Kerren offers helpful tips in this discussion forum topic: Vaccine Associated Sarcoma

I suggest that anyone who has any of these sarcomas diagnosed discuss the possibility of it being caused by a vaccine with their vet. Ask for the vaccine records for the vet to pursue reimbursement for treatment from the pharmaceutical company."
- MONA'S MOM, KERREN

The Basics About Injection-site Sarcomas in Cats

Up to 55 percent of cats with a vaccine lump will be diagnosed with a sarcoma tumor. Typically these tumors occur in the scruff of the neck, the scapula area, flank, paralumbar and femoral (thigh) regions of the leg.

These tumors are commonly diagnosed in cats ranging from 6 to 7 years old or ten to eleven years. Up to 22,000 new cases of vaccine associated sarcomas develop annually and about 80 percent of these sarcomas are reported as fibrosarcoma growths. All breeds are susceptible to this condition.

In a 2013 paper entitled "Feline Vaccine-Associated Sarcoma" Dr. Dennis W. Macy DVM, MS, DACVIM, Professor Emeritus at the Colorado State University College of Veterinary Medicine provides a synopsis of existing research about this condition. Today, the condition is known as "Feline Injection Site Sarcoma (FISS). Dr. Macy's paper states that:

...the association between sites of vaccine administration and subsequent development of high-grade sarcomas and other mesenchymal tumors in cats has been well documented and accepted by the veterinary community."
- DR. MACY

Suspected Causes of FISS

Dr. Macy reports that researchers suspect that "chronic inflammation associated with adjuvant most often included in rabies and feline leukemia virus vaccines (typically aluminum) may play a role in the development of vaccine associated sarcomas." Sometimes injection-site tumors develop even when a cat is given other types of vaccine, although evidence is slim at this point.

Chronic inflammation is strongly suspected to be a culprit in any cancer tumor growth and its role in vaccines is apparent.

In addition to reactions of vaccine adjuvants (the ingredient of a vaccine that helps create a stronger immune response in the patient's body), veterinary scientists also hypothesize that skin inflammation resulting from trauma at the injection site may cause a tumor to develop.

> *Trauma associated with the injection process, including muscle tearing or the introduction of hair into the subcutaneous tissues at the time of injection, can result in inflammation," writes Dr. Macy. "In light of these observations, injection-site sarcomas (ISS) may be a more accurate descriptive term for these tumors,*
> – DR. MACY

Current FISS Research

The latest guidelines, "<u>Feline Injection Site Sarcomas (FISS): Risk Factors, Diagnosis, Staging, and Treatment Algorithm</u>," state:

> *Any sarcoma arising in the vicinity of a known injection site should be considered a FISS and treated aggressively. Treatment is challenging because tumors are locally invasive and recurrence rates approach 70%, especially in the absence of radical surgical procedures.9 For this reason, first-line therapy for FISS is aggressive radical surgery. Adjunctive therapies, such as pre- or postoperative radiation or chemotherapy, depend on the histologic features of the tumor, completeness of excision, and clinical status of the patient.*

If your cat is suspected to have FISS, the paper goes on to explain that if a tumor excision is chosen over amputation, the surgery should be done by an experienced surgeon:

> *FISS are locally invasive tumors and as such should be treated aggressively. The best outcomes are obtained when an initial radical surgical excision is performed by a surgical specialist. Many cases are optimally treated with multi-modal therapy, including surgery, radiation therapy, and chemotherapy. Despite aggressive measures, local treatment failure leading to humane euthanasia within 2 to 3 months of recurrence is the most common cause of death in cats with FISS.*

What FISS Diagnosis and Treatment Might Look Like

If your vet suspects your cat has an Injection Site Sarcoma, a fine needle aspirate of the tumor will be performed. Should it come back positive for FISS, x-rays are recommended to determine if the cancer has metastasized.

Advanced imagine is also recommended before surgery. Ultrasound, computerized tomography (CT) and magnetic resonance imaging (MRI) provide a better understanding of the extent of the tumor growth. These tests also show if it is possible to surgically remove enough of the tumor and it's "tentacles" to avoid recurrence. CT scans and MRIs also outline the field of radiation therapy required for better odds at remission.

Pre-surgery treatment options sometimes include radiation therapy and chemotherapy. However the recurrence rate remains high even with these types of intervention. If your cat's FISS tumor is in the scapula, complete surgical removal is difficult even when performed by the best surgeons. Amputation offers a higher cure rate for these tumors than other types of therapies. However even with amputation, radiation therapy is usually advised afterward to ensure that the tumor's outgrowths are completely removed.

In this helpful report about Injection Site-Associated Sarcomas, the author Jane Ladlow explains:

> *...one would hope the current practice of interscapular injections will change, perhaps using the hind limbs rather than distal hind limbs as vaccination at the level of the stifle*

is tolerated by many cats and still allows good surgical margins with amputation if an injection site associated sarcoma develops. As a number of FISSs have also occurred following the administration of long-acting corticosteroids and long-acting penicillins, it would be good practice to avoid injecting these drugs into the scruff of the feline neck. Once this message pervades into general practice, we will hopefully improve the prognosis associated with these tumors.
– JANE LADLOW

In the Clinician's Brief article, "Feline Injection Site Sarcoma" author Dr. Sandra Axiak DVM DACVIM (Oncology) at the University of Missouri advises:

Overall, the results for treatment of ISS are disappointing. Local control is difficult to achieve, with the best results incorporating a combination of aggressive surgery and radiation therapy. The role of chemotherapy is undefined.

The most important aspects of treatment for good results are early identification of disease and advanced imaging and surgery at a referral institution. Current research is focused on immunotherapy and targeted therapy.
– DR. SANDRA AXIAK

! TIP: Once your cat's tumor has been histologically identified as an FISS tumor, ask your vet to report your case to the vaccine manufacturer as well as the U.S. Pharmacopoeia Veterinary Practitioners' Reporting Program. If your vet doesn't already have the information, have them request reporting forms at 800-4-USP-PRN (800-487-7776) or visit the USP Web site at www.usp.org.

Should My Family Vet Remove an Injection Site Sarcoma?

It seems logical that if there's a chance that a tumor resection (removal) surgery can cure the cancer, why not try that first? Starting with the least invasive surgical treatment for cancerous tumors seems to make sense. This is why your family vet may offer to perform a "tumor excision" (removal) surgery instead of amputation.

If your vet recommends a tumor excision, please keep in mind that when it comes to injection-site sarcomas, the risk of tumor recurrence may be greatest when a general practitioner performs the procedure.

In a 2011 report about injection site sarcomas in cats, veterinary oncologist Heather M. Wilson-Robles, DVM, DACVIM-ONC explains that on average, when general practitioners remove injection-site sarcomas the patient will only have a disease free interval (DFI) time of just 66 days after removal. However when a boarded surgeon removes the sarcoma, on average these cats enjoy a DFI of 274 days before tumor recurrence.

"The first surgery is the best chance to achieve long term survival. Disease free intervals (DFI) go down with marginal surgeries and repeated surgeries," Dr. Wilson-Robles says. And Dr. Sue Cancer Vet concurs, "You want your first surgery to be your only surgery,"

Diagnosing Cancer in Cats

Whatever type of cancer is suspected, it's important to determine the type of tumor so your vet can present appropriate treatment options.

Biopsy Basics

Diagnostics don't require you to pursue treatments, but they help you make an educated decision about which path you take. Pre-amputation diagnostic tests are critical for the health and even life of your cat. These tests can reveal if metastasis has occurred and the tumor type and aggressiveness, as well as the precise location.

Aside from determining the kind of cancer your pet has, diagnostics can also:
- Identify any medical conditions that haven't manifested in the past
- Reveal any medical conditions that aren't visible with a physical exam
- Predict your cat's anesthetic risk.

Your vet will want to perform a biopsy, which removes tissues from the area of a suspected cancerous tumor. The sample helps define the types of cells present, reveal if they are cancerous and sometimes define the aggressiveness of the cancer itself. A pathologist will double-check the results and then share with your vet who can then recommend treatment options. There are two kinds of biopsies that can help you get there.

Fine Needle Biopsy

The preferred biopsy method for diagnosing appendicular tumors is called a "fine (closed) needle aspirate" (FNA) biopsy. A fine needle aspirate biopsy is a quick, in-office procedure that takes a small sample from the suspected tumor. This simple biopsy can detect up to 94 percent of cancers. Plus, if a bone tumor is involved, this procedure has little risk of a pathological fracture. The patient usually only needs a sedative and local anesthesia for the procedure which results in little pain afterward.

Open Incisional Biopsy

A more invasive bone biopsy, known as an "open incisional biopsy" is a general anesthesia procedure that takes several large core samples from the affected area. Because it's a surgery, your cat will need pre-op blood work and diagnostics for this test.

Keep in mind that if your cat has a bone tumor, this is a highly painful procedure that literally punches a hole in the bone. Most vet experts feel this procedure is unnecessary and less advantageous than a fine needle aspirate biopsy if evidence of a cancerous tumor is strong. An open incisional biopsy's success rate at diagnosing an exact type of cancer is actually less than a closed needle biopsy, and it can cause complications such as hematoma, infection, dehiscence, tumor seeding, and pathologic fracture.

Are Bone Biopsies Necessary?

Bone biopsies can help determine what kind of cancer your cat has, and what kind of treatment is best if you are considering chemotherapy. But bone biopsies are not necessary if the bone is destroyed and you will amputate regardless of the diagnosis. This is especially true if you are not considering cancer care like chemotherapy. If you are considering amputation you may want to spare your cat the pain of this extra procedure. Your vet can conduct the open incisional biopsy after the leg is removed.

After the Biopsy

If the lab results indicate your cat has cancer, your vet may refer you to a veterinary cancer specialty center where other diagnostics will be performed, such as additional radiographs (x-rays), MRI or CT scans and possibly an ultrasound. Your vet may also recommend another fine needle aspirate at local lymph nodes near the tumor.

If the lymph nodes show cancer metastasis, it can determine the entire course of treatment and sometimes even rule it out altogether if a short prognosis is suspected. "A lymph node positive is a red light for surgery with osteosarcoma," says Dr. Phillip Bergman, DVM, MS, PhD, DACVIM (Oncology) . "It's rare when it does happen like that but when it does, it's a less than 60-day survival odds."

All diagnostic tests your vet recommends will "stage" the cancer by showing how far the cancer has spread and if other parts of the body are involved. Many general practice vets can stage cancer but we recommend working with a cancer specialist if you can. Veterinary oncologists are always up on the latest procedures and therapies.

If you are comfortable with your family vet handling your cat's treatments, you can feel more confident about their capabilities by trying to determine if the vet has a strong interest in treating cancer. You also want to make sure the vet has invested in the latest surgery and oncology equipment and protocols. Start your investigation by asking questions such as:

- How long have you been treating patients with chemotherapy?
- How often do you treat each month? Is it something you enjoy doing?
- Can I talk to a few of your oncology clients?
- What kind of safety measures do you have in place for my cat and your staff?

"I'm a sincere believer that primary care veterinarians can do chemotherapy as well as I can," says Dr. Bergman, one of the leading vet oncologists in North America. The veterinarians he feels confident about handling chemotherapy are those who are very interested and immersed in oncology. "They're what I call an 'onco groupie,' he explained in a 2015 American Animal Hospital Association presentation. "They take everything in from the literature that they can. Those are the people that I trust."

Cat Cancer Oncology Treatments

The vet you choose for care can give you a better idea of treatment options. Treating cancer in animals or humans usually consists of three general methods:
- Surgery
- Chemotherapy
- Radiation

The recommended treatment depends on several factors such as tumor location and aggressiveness or "stage" of the tumor. Where you live can also influence what treatments are recommended, their associated costs and ultimately, what you can afford will also impact your decision.

> *Although the optimal combination of radiation therapy and surgery is not known, the above results suggest that many soft tissue sarcomas that are not or cannot be completely excised can be controlled for a significant amount of time with the multimodality approach of surgery and radiation therapy. With more frequent use of the grading system for soft tissue sarcomas, more complete information about risk of metastasis and long term prognosis may help owners make the best decision about their treatment options.*
> – DR. NICOLE EHRHART, VMD, MS, DIPLOMATE ACVS

Surgery (Amputation)

If prior attempts to remove your cat's limb tumor are unsuccessful, amputation surgery is often the next course of action for cats who are considered to be good candidates for the procedure. Sometimes amputation will eliminate the cancer altogether and other times it is done to provide pain relief and offer a better quality of life. Other treatments are often recommended to enhance the pain relief benefits of amputation. These treatments often include chemotherapy or radiation treatments.

Chemotherapy

Amputation alone sometimes doesn't help the patient reach the goal of remission. That's when other treatments like chemotherapy and radiation therapy may help. Chemotherapy drugs aim to kill cancer cells while sparing healthy ones. It's a straightforward procedure but the thought of putting a cat through cancer therapy can be scary.

Words like "radiation" and "chemotherapy" might conjure up images of day-glow cats and traumatic day-long visits to the vet's office. But rest assured, it's well known in the vet community that pets usually suffer fewer side effects than humans. As a bonus, they also bounce back faster from treatments. This is because the goal of pet cancer oncology is completely different than it is in humans.

Why Cats Do Better with Chemo Than Humans

Since pets have much shorter life expediencies than humans, the goal of veterinary chemotherapy is to achieve remission (cancer slow-down) through lower drug doses and fewer treatments. This allows for a good quality of life in whatever time they would naturally have left with us before cancer entered the picture.

Oncology for humans, however, aims for total cancer obliteration through longer, more intense treatments. As a result, most pets usually don't endure the same harsh cancer treatment side effects that people encounter, such as hair loss and nausea. In most cases for pets, side effects are easily handled by prescription drugs. Few need cats hospitalization due to these effects.

If your veterinarian feels your cat may benefit from chemotherapy, your cat will be carefully screened to make sure her health is strong enough to withstand chemotherapy drugs. Cats with pre-existing kidney issues will be given extra consideration when it comes to the type of treatment being administered.

What Does Cat Cancer Treatment Look Like?

The type of chemotherapy drug your veterinary oncologist recommends will depend on the staging results of your cat's cancer as well as their own success rate with certain therapies. Most drugs are usually given intravenously in the office, but sometimes delivered in pill form or occasionally injected directly into the tumor during an in-office procedure.

Chemotherapy for animals isn't nearly as bad as we imagine it to be. Most pets handle it better than we assume they will. If your cat is comfortable at the vet's office and you can afford treatment, chemotherapy is usually a no-brainer.

! TIP: Chemotherapy has many benefits, but it's not a requirement for a successful outcome.

You always have the choice to skip it and hope for the best after amputation. Or you can try it, and stop if you don't like how it's affecting your cat.

Even with chemotherapy, no treatment can guarantee your cat will live up to or beyond the prognosis. Although statistics often show that animals who receive chemo have a better chance of living longer, chemotherapy is still a gamble. We've seen the results of this treatment go either way in our community. Some pets outlive their prognosis with chemotherapy. Others don't live anywhere near that time frame. Some who didn't have chemo at all will still outlive the worst-case prognosis!

What it amounts to is that your cat doesn't have an expiration date stamped on her butt. With or without cancer and with or without chemo, nobody can predict the future. If you are able to pay for chemotherapy and want to give it a shot, that's awesome! If it is not an option for you, please don't feel bad. Many Tripawds members skip it and nobody in our community will judge you for doing so.

Types of Radiation Therapy

Radiation therapy is another treatment veterinary oncologists may suggest to enhance the effects of amputation surgery, or provide pain relief if amputation isn't an option. Two types of radiation therapy long used in human medicine are now performed on pets in a growing number of cities with veterinary oncology practices. An overview of these treatments follows.

Conventional Radiation Therapy

Similar to an x-ray machine, conventional radiation therapy uses a machine called a 'linear accelerator' to deliver a concentrated beam of radiation that's strong enough to kill cancer cells while doing little harm to surrounding cells. Depending on the type of cancer being treated, this type of therapy usually requires 15-21 treatment sessions over 3-7 weeks. Other than the anesthesia risk, skin irritation or hair loss, this carries few side effects for patients.

Stereotactic Radiation Therapy

Also known as "cyberknife" therapy, stereotactic radiation

therapy (SRT) is a much more targeted form of radiation therapy that only requires only 1-3 treatments to treat and sometimes eradicate cancerous cells without harming surrounding tissues. With fewer treatments, patients endure less anesthesia and have less chance of side effects. With equipment costs in the millions of dollars, this type of therapy is mostly available at large veterinary teaching hospitals and through veterinary oncology service providers like <u>Pet Cure</u> locations.

Radixact radiation therapy

This new mind-blowing pet cancer radiation treatment is available at the <u>University of Wisconsin</u>, and hopefully coming to other clinics soon. Known as "adaptive radiotherapy," it uses a process called "real-time motion tracking" to stay zeroed in on the tumors and zap them, even when a patient's body moves as they inhale and exhale to breathe.

The Radixact is a huge win for the cat or dog with cancer. In the past, pets who had tumors in hard to reach locations could not get treatment. But thanks to this new technology, they can. This is the biggest breakthrough in pet cancer treatment that we've seen in a while.

Immunotherapy: an Exciting Advancement in Veterinary Oncology

Cancer research makes new discoveries all the time. One of the most promising ones is <u>immunotherapy</u>. This type of cancer treatment stimulates the patient's own immune system in order to target and kill cancer cells in the body.

You may have heard about the <u>Canine Osteosarcoma Vaccine</u>, which is one type of immunotherapy. This relatively new treatment has few side effects and is easier on the body than conventional cancer treatments like chemotherapy. Other therapies like the <u>Torigen vaccine</u> and <u>ELIAS vaccine</u> are also making inroads to treating and eradicating cancer in pets. Immunotherapy is gaining traction as more research gets published by veterinary teaching institutions. More treatments are in the works for feline patients specifically.

Your cat may be a candidate for a current immunotherapy clinical trial that pays for treatments in order to study how it helps fight cancer. To find a trial near you, see:

- [Comparative Oncology Clinical Trials Consortium](#)
- [AVMA Health Studies Database of Clinical Trials](#)

Ask an Oncologist: What to Expect When Treating Cat Cancer

Are you unsure about treating cancer in your cat? You're not alone. Until recently, treating cat cancer wasn't on the radar for many people. Today the number of cats being treated is rising, but feline oncology is relatively new in the world of veterinary medicine. The downside is that there are few studies about how cats handle treatment, the success rate of different therapies, side effects and more.

You may feel like you're all alone in considering treatment. The truth however, is that many cat parents have taken this path. Should you decide to pursue treatment for your cat, you will join these trailblazers of feline oncology. Consider starting a free Tripawds blog so that other cat parents will find inspiration and hope in your cat's journey.

Q&A With a Cat Cancer Oncologist

In the Tripawds News blog article "Cat Cancer, Oncology and Radiation Realities", we asked Dr. Sonia Honkisz of the Michigan State University Veterinary Medical Center's Oncology Service to help us understand what to expect when treating cat cancer with chemotherapy or radiation.

Here's what we learned from our Q&A with Dr. Honkisz:

Q: What are some common limb cancers that call for chemotherapy treatments?

The most common cancer affecting the limb of a cat that we see is a soft tissue sarcoma, which are typically injection site or vaccine associated sarcomas. Depending on the patient, amputation may be the only treatment that is needed if complete excision of the tumor can be achieved and metastatic disease is not yet present.

Unfortunately, complete excision is often not possible due to the size of the tumor at the time of presentation and diagnosis. In these patients, we then use either a combination of chemotherapy and radiation therapy or one of these treatments alone based on the location of the tumor and whether or not metastatic disease is present.

Any patient (cat or dog) that has cancer of its limb with metastatic disease should be treated with chemotherapy as long as the owners are willing and able to pursue such treatment. One of the main reasons to treat any patient with chemotherapy is due to the presence of metastatic disease or the high likelihood of metastatic disease developing.

Q: In your experience, how well do cats handle chemotherapy? Do most cats do alright? What are some treatment challenges that are unique to cats?

The majority of cats tolerate chemotherapy quite well in my experience. The goal with any patient (cat or dog) receiving chemotherapy is to maintain or improve the patient's quality of life. If a patient is feeling sick because of his/her cancer, then chemotherapy should restore that patient's quality of life by treating the cancer and thus the ultimate cause of why the patient feels sick.

Ideally, the chemotherapy administered will return each patient's quality of life back to 100%. Sadly, this does not always happen since sometimes the cancer only partially responds to chemotherapy or does not respond at all. If the cancer only partially responds to treatment with chemotherapy, then those patients will likely only experience a partial return to what their quality of life once was.

Cats are unique in that they have different side effects to certain chemotherapy agents compared to dogs. Cats are also challenging in that the exact dose of certain chemotherapy drugs is not always known. This stems from the fact that we don't treat as many cats with chemotherapy, or with cancer in general, as we do dogs. Thus the number of studies on the dose and response to chemotherapy in cats are low compared to what has been published in dogs. The only way to remedy this is to treat more cats with different types of cancers, so we can learn from these patients.

Q: When it comes to radiation therapy, do cats handle it similarly to chemo? If not, how is it different?

Cats often handle radiation therapy better than chemotherapy. This is because radiation therapy treats a targeted area as opposed to chemotherapy, which is a systemic treatment meaning it goes everywhere in the body. With radiation therapy, we can target just the tumor and the surrounding affected tissues. As a result, the side effects experienced by the patient are limited to the area that is being treated.

One thing to remember with radiation therapy is that a patient must be placed under general anesthesia for each treatment. This ensures the patient remains still for each treatment, which allows only the area affected by the tumor to receive the full dose of radiation and spares all of the normal surrounding tissues.

With chemotherapy, the drug is most often given either orally or intravenously and travels via the blood stream throughout the body. If we could somehow tell the chemotherapy the exact locations we wanted it to go to that would be wonderful, but unfortunately that is not currently possible.

Q: What is the number one thing you want cat owners to know if their oncologist has recommended chemotherapy?

The most important thing for any cat (or dog) owner to know if chemotherapy is recommended by a veterinary oncologist to treat their pet's cancer is that we do not treat pets like people when it comes to cancer. For pets, it is all about quality of life. The reason for this is that unfortunately we cannot cure the majority of our patients of their cancer. Instead the goal is to give each patient the best quality of life possible for as long as possible by putting the cancer into some form of remission. As long as the cancer is responding and the patient is enjoying a good quality of life, then we will continue with that treatment. If the cancer is not responding or quality of life is not where it should be, then we can try a different chemotherapy agent or stop treatment at anytime."

When Amputation Is Not an Option for Cancer Treatment

Sometimes amputation just isn't an option for some cats. If you find yourself in this situation, don't despair. First, we encourage you to get at least one other opinion from an orthopedic specialist. Multiple opinions (such as from the family vet, an orthopedic specialist and an oncologist) can make all the difference for your cat.

All three may or may not agree about your cat's future on three legs. Or, maybe they will. Either way, getting multiple opinions has helped many Tripawds go on to live happy lives despite that first bleak assessment.

If you've covered your bases and you know in your heart that your cat is not a candidate for amputation, that's OK. We welcome you to be a part of our community anyways as an "Honorary Tripawd." You still have other options for treating cat cancer without amputation surgery.

Limb Salvage

Limb sparing (also known as limb salvage) is a surgical procedure that provides an alternative to amputation in selected pets being treated for bone tumors. It is often considered for pets with osteosarcoma who have concurrent orthopedic problems, such as severe arthritis, that might not do as well on three legs. The goal of this procedure is to remove the diseased bone and surrounding tissues and replace it with an implant that works in place of the bone to preserve the function of the remaining limb. Limb sparing is performed in conjunction with chemotherapy (and in some instances, radiation therapy as well).

One of the most well-known feline limb salvage patients was Cyrano the Cat. He wasn't a candidate for amputation so his people opted for a "limb sparing" procedure.

Surgical oncologists are testing new limb sparing treatments all the time. For example, Dr. Sarah Boston, DVM DVSc Diplomate ACVS has pioneered this procedure known as "limb shortening". The technique currently being performed only on dogs but could eventually translate to cats.

And as of 2022, a new treatment called cementoplasty is offering an amputation alternative for all pets with inoperable limb cancers.

Not every pet is a candidate for limb sparing. For those who are, Colorado State University's Flint Animal Cancer Center says that out of 300 limb salvage surgeries, about 85% of patients experience good to excellent function after the procedure.

Still thinking about limb sparing?

If you decide to pursue a limb salvage procedure for your cat you should know that infection rates remain high. This can lead to expensive complications that ultimately require amputation. The procedure is largely successful in humans but still being perfected in pets. It requires a tremendous amount of skill to execute. To be successful, limb sparing also needs the best in veterinary surgical technologies and protocols. Most general practice vets don't perform the procedure so a surgical oncologist is your best bet for success. If you are considering it, <u>contact your nearest veterinary teaching hospital</u> to inquire about availability in your region.

A New Type of Limb Sparing and Pain Relief Option

In 2022, a new cancer therapy for pets with bone cancer was released in the U.S. and Europe. This <u>cementoplasty</u> treatment can be given to pets with osteosarcoma, as a palliative treatment when amputation is not ideal. In <u>this Tripawd Talk Radio episode</u>, BIOCERA-VET explains how it's a minimally invasive injection into the affected bone that has been weakened by a tumor.

BIOCERA-VET studies show that the treatment reduces the risk of pathologic fracture, relieves pain and improves patient comfort and quality of life.

Palliative Care

Limb cancers can be aggressive and unpredictable. If the cancer has already shown signs of metastasizing elsewhere in the body, then palliative care may be the best course of treatment, instead of amputation.

Palliative care uses a combination of radiation therapy, immunotherapy and pharmaceutical drug therapies to manage pain resulting from the cancerous bone tumor. Many times the cancer can be managed for a limited amount of time, anywhere from six months to a year depending on the aggressiveness of the disease. Some cats can go many months without vocally expressing any symptoms of pain.

The experts at Mar Vista Animal Medical Center want you to know:

> *No single medication, however, is a match for the pain involved in what amounts to a slowly exploding bone. A combination of medications is needed to be reasonably palliative and should be considered only as a last resort if amputation or radiation therapy will not be pursued.*
>
> – <u>MAR VISTA ANIMAL MEDICAL CENTER</u>

Bisphosphonates for Limb Tumor Pain Management

Current pain management therapies can also include bisphosphonates. This is a bone-building drug prescribed to humans with conditions like osteoporosis, which has also been proven to have pain management properties. Pamidronate is one treatment, several others exist.

One of our favorite veterinary oncologists Dr. Jeannette Kelly says:

> *It (bisphosphonates) help relieve their discomfort and bone pain is a horrible type of pain and there's only so much you can do with non-steroidals or morphine types of drugs and a bisphosphonate and we do know that bisphosphonates can help build bone, strengthen the bone.*
>
> *We do know that it has anti-cancer properties as well. They've shown that in the petri plate. So it's – it can hurt the kidneys and you can have side effects. We don't see side effects. So we use it regularly and people's dogs can do what they like to do when they're on Zoledronate.*

Research behind bisphosphonates for feline bone tumors is slim. But while searching for palliative care pain management of feline bone cancers, we came across these studies about bisphosphonates for cats with bone cancers:

- Pamidronate Disodium for Palliative Therapy of Feline Bone-Invasive Tumors
- Medication-related osteonecrosis of the jaw after long-term bisphosphonate treatment in a cat

What About "Natural" Medicine?

None of us want to give harsh chemicals to our pets. Using natural remedies seems like a smart choice. If you want to explore what is now called "integrative" medicine, extra homework is necessary for this unconventional choice.

Not all veterinarians who practice conventional medicine will be against your desire to mix natural remedies with conventional palliative cancer treatments. In Southern California, Dr. Johnny

Chretin, head of oncology at VCA Animal Hospital West Los Angeles is an advocate of integrative treatments. Dr. Chretin doesn't discourage parents from pursuing this type of care, provided that they are talking to a qualified practitioner. He also urges parents to remain aware that these remedies cannot replace what western medicine does.

"Any good holistic practitioner is going to tell an owner what they can offer, not replace what western medicine does," he explains in our [interview about treating cancer with holistic medicine](#).

If natural cancer therapy sounds interesting, talk to a vet about it first. Many vets are willing to help you balance complimentary therapies with conventional medicine to help your cat thrive. Keep an open mind. Talk to practitioners of both western and alternative medicines before investing in any therapies.

Recommended Reading:
- Extensive reading lists with links to related articles and videos are available in the Premium E-book. **Save $5 OFF with coupon code: BASIC5**
https://tri.pet/tricatbook

CHAPTER 3:
Is Your Vet Qualified?

The Medical Team: What to Look for in a Practice

If you feel like amputation is a good option, then ask yourself: "What are my vet's qualifications to do the surgery?"

Not all vet practices can do everything, especially when it comes to a major surgery like amputation. Your family vet might have the technical know-how, but the practice itself might not have the equipment and staff to address unexpected problems.

For many of us, the decision to amputate is the first time we investigate the surgical capabilities of our chosen vet practice. Start with these tips and suggestions before deciding.

Step 1: Advocate to Get the Best Care for Your Cat

Do you zone out when your vet starts explaining things to you? Most people are intimidated by a doctor's white coat. If you have "white coat syndrome," your pets might not get the best care that they deserve. Author and veterinarian Dr. Nancy Kay explains it best:

> *I'm referring to what is known as the "white coat intimidation factor; a phenomenon that gives the doctor an air of authority and superiority. When she is on such a "pedestal," two-way communication flounders. Medical advocacy requires active client participation, and a client who is intimidated does not feel comfortable voicing an opinion.*
> – DR. NANCY KAY, TWELVE THINGS TO EXPECT FROM YOUR VET

Our pets need us to stop being intimidated by medical providers. Start by keeping lines of communication open. The ability to talk with and be heard by our vets is how we get information that allows us to make informed choices about our animals' care.

The best way to help pets get quality care is to work with a vet who practices "relationship centered care." Dr. Kay describes these vets as follows:

> *...recognize that their responsibilities expand beyond their patients to include the emotional well-being of their clients. They are willing to be a source of empathy and support. Vets who are oriented towards relationship centered care believe in collaborative decision-making. Rather than telling their clients what to do, they make recommendations, and then ask for feedback, questions and concerns.*

How do you know if you have a relationship centered vet?

- Your vet doesn't roll their eyes when you mention that you've been researching online.
- Your vet addresses all of your concerns about different aspects of your pet's care
- Your vet listens to you carefully before suggesting a treatment.
- Relationship centered vets don't hesitate to offer an outside referral for a second opinion. One sign of a great vet is they know when to ask for input from a specialist.

Twelve Things to Expect From Your Vet

According to Dr. Kay, there are 12 primary elements of a good veterinary team. When choosing the veterinarian who will handle your cat's amputation surgery, don't ignore these twelve important clues:

- Practice relationship centered care
- Provide round-the-clock care
- Give clients access to "the back" of the hospital
- Present all treatment options regardless of cost
- Offer written cost estimates
- Promptly provide referrals for second opinions and specialized care
- Will tailor vaccinations to your pet's health and your concerns
- Are open to talking about your pet' diet
- Will listen to your internet research discoveries
- Allow email communications
- Offer visitation hours when your cat is hospitalized
- Will provide a safe place to be with your cat at the very end of her life

Signs of a Great Vet Practice Include:
- Spotless facilities
- Trained in <u>fear-free handling procedures</u>
- Provide detailed cost estimates before a procedure
- Keep you updated when your cat is left at the clinic for care
- Allow you to be present during basic procedures
- Give you thorough explanations of potential treatments, regardless of cost

Step 2: Find a Cat Friendly Practice

Cats are no longer second class citizens in a growing number of clinics, thanks to the American Association of Feline Practitioners (AAFP) and the International Society for Feline Medicine (ISFM). Together these two organizations have created the <u>Cat Friendly Practice</u>® Program, a worldwide educational campaign for vets to implement in order to reduce vet visit stress for cats, their caregivers and their veterinary team.

Working with a Cat Friendly Practice is so important during this stressful time. According to the <u>American Association of Feline Practitioners</u> website, you and your cat can experience more relaxed vet visits when working with these clinicians because their clinics feature the following:
- Calming environments.
- Waiting areas that reduce the stressors caused by other pets and odd vet clinic smells.
- Surgery, recovery and hospitalization areas with equipment, tools and procedures specific to cats.
- Feline-only examination rooms with a non-threatening environment, so cats can be examined calmly and effectively.

Want more proof about why choosing a Cat Friendly Practice is so important?
- Take a minute to watch this <u>Cat Friendly Practice video</u>.
- Or download this brochure: <u>What to look for in a cat-friendly practice</u>.

"The NOTABLE differences are the Quality of Care. Time spent at appt, dealing with cat-specific issues and follow-ups! Genuinely caring about your cat and want the best for them in the future. MASSIVE!
– <u>PURRKINS NEW CAT FRIENDLY PRACTICE</u>

IS YOUR VET QUALIFIED?
Look for Fear Free Vets!

In addition to Cat Friendly Practices we encourage you to seek out vet clinics following Dr. Marty Becker's Fear Free initiative. This program trains veterinary professionals to help them remove the fear, anxiety and stress from vet clinic visits. Fear Free certified vets, technicians, and other pet professionals like groomers understand how to enhance the physical and emotional well-being of your pets both during and after a visit. As Dr. Becker stays, the program "aims to take the pet out of petrified."

Step 3: Find out if your clinic meets modern standards.

In addition to caring for the emotional well-being of your cat during this procedure, take time to ensure the practice you choose meets modern standards for care. Amputation surgery requires a clinic to be current in the areas of equipment, anesthesia, sterilization and after care procedures.

! DID YOU KNOW: Veterinary practice accreditation is entirely voluntary! Human hospitals must meet accreditation standards set by certain agencies in order to practice medicine, but not vet clinics.

The best way to find a clinic with the most modern and safe care is to seek out a hospital accredited by the American Animal Hospital Association (AAHA).

This organization is the only one in North America that accredits veterinary hospitals in the United States and Canada. A practice accredited by the American Animal Hospital Association (AAHA) has met stringent standards of care, utilizes modern equipment and employs trained staff.

AAHA-accredited clinics have passed a rigorous accreditation process that better protects the health of animals. Every three years, AAHA clinics must pass rigorous standards in these areas:
- Emergency Services
- Pain Management
- Contagious Diseases
- Surgery and Anesthesia
- Radiology Services
- Pathology Services
- Nursing Care
- Diagnostic and Pharmacy

HOW TO HELP YOUR THREE LEGGED CAT

- Dentistry
- Examination Facilities
- Pet Medical Records
- Medical Library
- Housekeeping and Maintenance

At an AAHA clinic, everyone there makes sure your Tripawd has the best vet care possible.

Through the years our community has occasionally experienced tragic endings to members' amputation surgeries. Examples include life-ending blood clots to MRSA infections to horrific, painful post-op care. Each time, we couldn't help but wonder if those members' clinics were AAHA-certified. We can't say for sure if being AAHA-accredited could have made a difference, but why take a chance?

- Find out if your clinic is AAHA-accredited!

Questions to Ask Your Vet About Amputation Surgery and Care

When amputation is recommended by a veterinarian, it's important to feel confident that the vet can handle a major surgery in their clinic. Even if you already have a veterinarian you trust, there are important things to consider prior to surgery that can mean the difference between life and death. This useful Guide to Veterinary Surgery lists the most important things to investigate in a clinic. Make time to ask your vet important questions such as:

Q: How often do you perform amputations?

If you choose a board certified surgeon with the "ACVS" letters after their name, you know your cat is in good hands. Boarded vet surgeons have the latest training in veterinary surgery. That's not to say a family vet cannot do amputation surgery well, because many do. Lots of Tripawds had great experiences when a family vet did their surgery. Their humans saved a lot of money too, since ACVS surgeons understandably charge higher fees for their advanced knowledge.

But for your cat's safety, you want to make sure that a non-boarded vet does a lot of amputations each year. To find out about your vet's experience, just ask, "How often do you do amputation surgeries?" You're looking for a vet with lots of practice.

Q: Will you refer me to a specialist if things get complicated?

Your vet should be willing to refer you to a specialist if additional diagnostics are needed. Or, if recovery gets too complicated for the level of care they can provide. That doesn't mean you'll need to abandon your relationship with that primary vet. They will be your liaison during the time your cat needs specialty help.

Q: Will my cat have 24/7 care?

Did you know that not all vets provide overnight care? When cats need overnight hospitalization, having trained staff at night can mean the difference between a smooth recovery and serious complications that go undetected for hours. Although rare, some Tripawd parents have called the vet's office the morning after a successful surgery, only to find out that their beloved pet died sometime during the night. Nobody noticed the patient wasn't doing well, because nobody was at the clinic!

Large vet practices usually have certified medical staff that check on patients at night. They charge more for the ability to provide that service. High quality, small practices will have arrangements with larger facilities that have a certified veterinary technician stop by throughout the night to check on patients. They might also have an arrangement with a 24-hour care provider who monitors patients in their facility at night, then returns them in the morning.

> ! TIP: Do not leave your cat alone overnight in a clinic without 24/7 supervision! There have been some Tripawds who might not have died during recovery if someone had been there at night to monitor them closely.

Q: Do you use feline-friendly anesthesia techniques?

You'll want to make sure your vet is <u>minimizing the risks of anesthesia in feline patients</u> is critical.

> *Approximately one in 1,000 healthy cats and one in 2,000 healthy dogs die under anesthesia each year. While any anesthetic-related deaths are unacceptable, these incidence rates are actually quite low. But of course, there's still plenty of room for improvement. One of the reasons we still see*

deaths related to anesthetic procedures is because not all practices are actively taking all of the steps necessary to reduce anesthetic risk."
- HEIDI SHAFFORD, DVM, PHD, DACVA

In these helpful <u>pet parent tips about cats and anesthesia</u>, the American Animal Hospital Association says you can minimize anesthesia risk. Discuss your cat's behaviors that can affect recovery, such as:

- How is your cat's daily energy level? How well does she tolerate exercise?
- How often does she cough or sneeze? Any changes in her breathing?
- How often does she vomit?
- How much, how often, and what does she eat? Any changes?
- Has your pet ever had anesthesia before? What happened?
- What medical problems does she have?
- List all her prescription medications, supplements (including cannabidiol, aka CBD), and over-the-counter medications. Which ones has he taken in the last 24 hours?
- Has your pet had any food or water today?
- What procedure is she having today?
- What concerns do you have?

Your veterinary anesthesia staff is trained to carefully select, dose, and administer medications, and to monitor your pet while they are at the hospital. But, a big part of the success of your pet's anesthetic procedure is up to you.
- AAHA GUIDELINES

Q: Are your veterinary techs licensed?

A veterinary technician plays a lifesaving roll in the medical procedure. Licensed technicians understand how to measure and administer drugs, place catheters and monitor animals under anesthesia. However, not all states require vet techs to be licensed. A growing number of vet practices do require their techs to be licensed. We think the more licensed technicians, the better off your pet will be.

To see if your state requires vet tech licensing, check the <u>American Association of Veterinary State Boards directory</u>. Ask your vet:
- ▶ Does your practice have licensed technicians?
- ▶ What kind of training do they get to care for pets after major surgery?
- ▶ How often they must take continuing education classes?

Q: What pain management protocols do you practice for amputation surgery?

Knowing how your veterinarian will handle pain control is vital to the recovery and happiness of your cat. Tripawds' resident vet, Dr. Pam Wiltzius of Puyallup, Washington, recommends asking about pain control before surgery day.

> *It used to be that pain was dealt with post-op, but a lot of pain can be prevented now by administering Gabapentin pre-op, using an MLK (morphine) drip during and after surgery, and performing nerve blocks intra-op.*
> – DR. PAM W. (AKA: TAZZIEDOG)

Sometimes there is a huge difference in pain protocols among vets – especially when it comes to feline patients. Some vets still don't adhere to the <u>latest veterinary pain management protocols</u>. Their patients often come home with just a few days of pain medications that aren't adequately controlling pain. However, cats whose vets practice current pain management procedures will receive anywhere from seven to 14 days of the most current pain control medications.

> *We noticed a big difference right away – they understand what pain signals your cat is experiencing & they treat accordingly. There is no begging for medicine and made to feel like your drug-seeking.*
>
> *I was not speaking a foreign language trying to explain what pain signals Purrkins was showing me! Never did I have to repeat or have the need to try to explain further!*
>
> *When I phoned the traditional vet to tell him the 1/4 capsule of Gaba was not helping Purrkins discomfort, he was hesitant to send more home.*
> – <u>PURRKINS NEW CAT FRIENDLY PRACTICE</u>

Good pain control leads to a better amputation recovery. Unmanaged pain will cause your cat to suffer through a longer, more difficult recuperation. Know where your vet stands on pain management.

Recommended Reading:
- Extensive reading lists with links to related articles and videos are available in the Premium E-book. **Save $5 OFF with coupon code: BASIC5**
https://tri.pet/tricatbook

IS YOUR VET QUALIFIED?

CHAPTER 4:
You Set the Tone for Surgery Recovery

Amputation is always harder on the humans than it is on the animal. Your own fear is a bigger obstacle than the surgery itself. If you decide to amputate, managing your mindset will be the key to getting your cat, your house, and everyone inside ready for the change.

<u>The Best Pet Amputation Recovery and Care Tips from Vets</u>
- Don't feel sorry for them.
- Practice patience. Remember that every day recovery gets better.
- Have a pawsitive attitude.
- Don't give up. They will get through it and YOU will get through it.
- Remember they'll recover and have a second lease on life!

Be a Good Leader

Cat's can't speak English but they understand our emotions – often better than we do. Before, during and after surgery, you must be a strong leader. Put aside any feelings of sadness or pity towards your cat.

Cats pick up on every emotion, so being positive will help her make the transition faster. Sure, it's difficult to watch your cat's first steps on three legs. We all cry tears of joy and sadness when we see it happen. But when you start to feel pity, remember that soon she will re-learn how to walk, go to the bathroom, and play on three legs. Recovery is only temporary.

Over time you will learn that pets don't feel sorry for themselves when they lose a leg, they're just glad to be out of pain. They just want to get on with the business of playing and living in the moment. Be sure to follow her lead.

Your Cat is Following Your Example

Animals can sense fear in humans and your cat is probably more upset by your worries than her own aches and pains. Every Tripawd parent feels overwhelmed, angry and scared at this time. And we know it's hard to think optimistically when it's clear that your cat's way of life will be altered forever, and you are faced with so much uncertainty.

But you must remember; you can't control the future, only how you react to the situation.

So, how will you spend these moments with your best friend? Calmly loving your cat and reassuring her that everything will be OK? Or crying and panicking while your cat hides under the bed? If you have to go outside for a good cry, do it, as long as you return with a smile on your face. Projecting confidence makes all the difference in the emotions your cat picks up on you.

> *I can't begin to describe how relieved I am! Nothing can prepare you for the emotional ride you go on. The fear, the guilt, the depression, the anxiety, the sadness, and the eventual, cautious joy in the little things, like coming out of the room and using the high sided litter box. Today, she started to run down the hall! Only 3 running hops before she slowed down again, but that made me so happy!*
>
> *We are still not fully out of the woods, because she still has that area of concern which gets a check up on Friday. So cross your fingers for no more procedures! I'm so grateful to you all here, for calming my fears, for being that sounding board. Thank you!*
>
> – @KIKI412

Stay Pawsitive

You can do lots of things to feel more upbeat. Take your focus off any grief and anger you may be feeling by following a few tips suggested by Drs. Demian Dressler DVM and Sue Ettinger, DVM DACVIM (authors of the <u>Dog Cancer Survival Guide</u>, as written for dog parents but definitely applicable to cat parents:

- ▶ Vent productively. To get the anger out of your system, try hard exercise or scream into a pillow, where your cat can't hear you. Vent until you're exhausted, and run out of steam.
- ▶ Learn gentle pet massage techniques

- Have a heart-to-heart with your cat, giving thanks for all she's brought into your life. Thank her for all the things that went right with her life and your time together, instead of focusing on what went wrong.
- Treat your cat's spirit as well as her mind; enhance your cat's quality of life by creating gentle change through things like varying your playtime activities or adding a special "cheat treat."
- Keep a journal or start a Tripawds Blog. This will allow you to review days and compare how your cat does from surgery day until the day she acts like herself again. A journal will help you make honest assessments of your Tripawd's progress during the ups and downs of recovery.

Let Go of Guilt, Regret and Shame

You're probably feeling guilty over making such a major decision for your cat, who doesn't understand what's about to happen (or why it did). But before guilt takes over, remember: animals aren't burdened with those silly human emotions of guilt, shame or regret. Those feelings are strictly a human thing. She's not wondering why her leg is gone; she's glad for the fact that she's out of pain.

When a three legged cat returns home to the pride, nobody says "Whoa! What happened to your leg?" They just get on with the business of being cats. After a cat loses a leg, all she wants is to recuperate so she can be herself again. Cats do not mourn the past, or feel ashamed for being different. Your cat will not hate you, or be angry.

When you pick her up from the hospital, she might appear confused, or fearful, and this will tear your heart out. But try to consider that any look of confusion or fear may indicate something entirely different. Your cat may appear to look that way only because she was so surprised she stayed overnight at the vet's, and those pain meds running through her system aren't making her depressed, they're causing her to see pink elephants!

Pain meds can cause odd behavior in just about every pet, which humans often think is depression. It's usually just medication side-effects.

YOU SET THE TONE FOR SURGERY RECOVERY

You'll feel like you made a mistake when you see your cat after surgery. Everyone does! But before you panic, ask yourself: how would you behave after surgery? Would you be yourself? Your cat may seem different but she's likely just exhausted, and a little confused. She will look to you for guidance.

Your job is to carry on and achieve a new normal that's pain-free and without worry, regret or fear. The sooner you can normalize life on three legs, the faster your cat will heal.

Mental Health Tips for tri-kitty Parents to Cope with Recovery

Consider the following to help manage the stress associated with your cat's amputation recovery and care:

- Remember you are helping your cat feel better. You are doing this for her, not to her!
- Be more cat! Think like a cat and live in the now.
- Always remember, animals don't know shame, regret or anger; your cat will not hate you.
- Don't overwhelm yourself with too much information or too many changes at once.
- All pets are different during recovery. What works for one may not work for another.
- The first two weeks after surgery are the hardest; arrange to be with your Tripawd for the first few days after she comes home; take time off if you are able.
- Sleep is medicinal and promotes healing. Let your cat rest as much as they want.
- Normalize life as soon as she comes home from the clinic. Try not to baby, carry, or sleep on the floor next to her. If you want life to be "normal" again, act as though it is normal.
- Celebrate each day you have together. Every minute is a blessing.
- If your family and friends are not supportive about your decision, it's probably best to avoid them during recovery. Post in the Three Legged Cats Forum for plenty of support from others who understand what you're going through.

Finally, remember to embrace all the little steps along the way. Because the greatest lesson you will learn from your cat during this experience is: enjoy the moment at hand, our time together today is really all we have.

Be More ~~Dog~~ Cat

We write about the many important life lessons <u>Tripawds Chief Fun Officer Jerry</u> taught us in our book, ***<u>Be More Dog: Learning to Live in the Now</u>***. **Resilience, acceptance, perseverance, adaptability**...these virtues are also possessed by all three legged cats. Follow their lead to enjoy a speedy recovery and happy life on three legs. Fans of Mooch in MUTTS comics will appreciate the illustration and <u>foreword by Patrick McDonnell</u>.

If you suspect your Tripawd is feeling down, these depression signs in otherwise healthy cats might confirm it:

- Not wanting to eat.
- Sleeping more than usual, tired.
- Clingy behavior.
- Extra vocal.
- Unusual and aggressive behavior.
- Hiding. (<u>Don't let new Tripawds under the bed!</u>)
- Toileting in unusual places.

If you feel as sad as your new Tripawd looks, that's to be expected. You may regret your decision to amputate, too. Those feelings are normal, everyone has them. But when recovery is over, any feelings of regret disappear for the majority of Tripawd parents.

For now, here's how to help a cat with depression.

- Call your vet. Share your cat's depression symptoms. Let them know you are concerned. A change in her pain medication schedule and dosages might be needed.
- Arrange a visit by your cat's favorite people. Spending quality time with someone your pet adores can make everyone happy.
- Play interactive brain games. Work your Tripawd's mind, not their body. Brain games tire out cats faster than zoomies around the house.

What to Expect During Recovery

Ask any Tripawd parent and they'll tell you: the first two weeks of recovery can be rough. One vet we interviewed, <u>Dr. Christine Hady of the Veterinary Emergency and Specialty Centers of New Mexico</u> (VESC), advises clients that post-amputation surgery recovery is similar to bringing home a new baby from the hospital. There are many sleepless nights but the experience is all worth it in the end!

When Your Cat Comes Home:

- Your cat's bodily functions will need monitoring, such as urination, defecating, breathing and appetite. Learn how to check your cat's vital signs at home.
- Remember that sleep will be a luxury; pain meds can make cats crazier than ever.
- Pain medication can cause a decreased appetite and constipation.
- Most cats will walk within 12 hours of surgery, but you may need to assist her in using the litterbox during the first week.
- Some cats will get a "seroma" or a fluid buildup at the surgery site. This is normal. It will drain pinkish (not bloody) fluid and be gross, but usually isn't a problem.
- Infections are rare, but they do happen. You'll be monitoring the surgery site to check for signs of infection and irritation.

While these aren't the only situations Tripawds encounter after amputation surgery, they are the most common post-op complications. If you are ever worried about your cat's post-surgery behavior, call your vet. Remember, that's why you pay them.

Things you can expect to do as your cat's nurse include:

- Using positive reinforcement to give your cat medication
- Creating an enclosed, secure place for administering medication. Try a closed bathroom where all supplies are within arms reach.
- Ensuring your cat eats and drinks. Use flat paper plates and shallow bowls for easier access.
- Observing your cat's fluid and food intake, urinating, bowel movements and behaviors. Watch for urination or constipation problems and monitor for any signs of internal illness like lethargy or diarrhea.

Every Cat is Different!

All cats are different in how they recuperate, but generally the amputation surgery recovery lasts anywhere from two to four weeks, and sometimes longer depending on the patient. Recovery time can also depend on any pre-existing health conditions. Many Tripawds will move around pretty normally within a week or two, but some take longer. Several weeks may pass before your Tripawd can build up more endurance to do what she loves best.

Accept that there will likely be challenges over the next few days that may make you sad, or even regret that you went through with the surgery. That's normal. Don't beat yourself up, you're doing what you think is best for your cat.

Remember to be strong, and know that the recovery time is just temporary. Don't get discouraged if you think progress is slow, and don't compare your cat's recovery with others you read about on Tripawds. She is her own unique self and will set her own recovery timeline.

Tips for Preparing Your Cat

Most Tripawds parents aren't prepared for the day their vet recommended amputation surgery. But you have the power to help your cat have an easier transition. Start by creating a Tripawd-friendly home with supplies like:
- Anti-slip floors
- Low sided litterboxes
- Raised food bowls

Be Prepared with the tri-kitty Pre-Surgery Shopping List

Certain supplies make the recovery phase much easier. Check out ideas in our <u>Tripawds Recovery Shopping List</u>. The cat-centric <u>Cat Amputation Recovery Shopping List</u> is especially helpful.

Cone of Shame Alternatives

Nobody has made a cone of shame recovery collar that cats don't mind wearing. See Chapter 7 for tips to use cones effectively. Meanwhile, if your pet has a reputation for outsmarting traditional e-collars, you may want to invest in one of the newer pet recovery collar alternatives such as:

- [Flower Pattern Soft e-Collar](#)
- [Comfy Cone Soft Pet Recovery Collar](#)
- [VetMedWear Amputation Recovery Suit for Cats and Dogs](#)

You can also make your own recovery suit! These [DIY Onesies for Cats](#) often work well for cats who won't wear a cone of shame.

Baby onesies (also called "Baby Grows" by our UK friends) are helpful for discouraging licking at the amputation incision even when a cone is worn. If your cat bothers the incision she can cause infection, pull stitches and end up back in the hospital. Don't let that happen. Ask your vet if it's OK to try this recovery tip before you actually do it. Purrkins' mom Holly did, and found that [Purrkins tolerated his baby onesies](#) quite well.

These [DIY pet surgery recovery suit](#) tips and are easy and inexpensive to try before surgery day.

> *The first challenge was what size do I buy? We looked at weight charts for baby onesies and I got 03-06 months based on the size chart for Purrkins. These worked but they were way too big and they shifted all over. Don't go by the weight chart this was not accurate for cats.*
> – HOLLY, PURRKINS MOM

Try a Low Sided Litter Box

Many new feline Tripawds have difficulty getting into and out of their usual litter box. This [Litterbox Tips for Cats](#) blog post shares how to make life easier after surgery.

See [what Molly's mom did for a litterbox](#). You can even [make your own DIY litterbox](#) for cats with extra challenges.

Keep recovery blankets, sheets and towels handy.

Sometimes body fluid leaks at the incision site. This is known as a [seroma](#). The drainage usually isn't a problem, but it can be messy. So keep your pet's bed covered. Disposable [pet wee pads](#) are best, but old towels can also be used too.

If a [seroma](#) occurs, let your vet know, and don't panic. Most go away on their own when the fluid is reabsorbed back into the body. Others may need to be drained by your vet which is a simple procedure.

Raise Your Cat's Food Bowls.

Animals eat standing up but when one leg is missing, it often makes balancing to drink and eat quite challenging. Raised feeders for pets help with better posture and stability while eating. These extra wide raised cat food bowls are a hit with Tripawd kitties.

Slip Proof Your Floors

No-slip rugs or yoga mats can give your Tripawd confidence by providing traction in your home. You don't have to cover entire home, just enough areas to create a path for your cat to navigate around their favorite places. They may not always use the covered areas but at least you'll know you're doing your best to help them avoid falls and injuries.

Stock up on canned food and irresistible treats.

Most recovering Tripawds have weak appetites, which is a common side effect of pain medication. This is about the only time it's perfectly OK to forget about calories and stock up on really tasty, tempting food to get your cat eating again.

▶ Churus are a great treat during recovery!

You may also want to spike your pet's water dish with yummy flavors like tuna water. This can encourage hydration. Being hydrated is important during recovery. It also helps cats avoid constipation, which is another common side effect of pain medication.

Preparing Your Other Cats for the New Tripawd

Animals smell things that we don't, and some of those smells come from the vet's office. From bandages to surgical drugs, animals can tell when one of their housemates has been to the clinic. When your new Tripawd comes home the vet clinic scent they carry may be overwhelming to other household cats.

A slow, careful introduction with other household cats is helpful for most cats. Your job is to monitor other cats' reactions to your new Tripawd. Prevent your recovering patient from getting too much activity too soon.

When you put all household members together, supervise until you are certain it's safe to leave them alone. In the Tripawds

Discussion Forum topic "How Did You Prepare Your Other Cats for the New tri-kitty?" members shared the following recovery experiences.

How did they react to your new tri-kitty?

mommatux said: "Initially Dazzle was very happy to see Tuxedo. He loved on him and helped groom him. Once the hard plastic cone of shame went on though, things changed. Dazzle would hiss & whack Tuxedo on the head (cone) whenever he got near. Though they were the bop and run type of thing. Dazzle never hung around him for long while the cone was in place. But he was continually watching and every time Tuxedo moved or made any sound he would come in for another try. I really think he was trying to help Tuxedo get the cone off on his own way, because as soon as Tuxedo got out of the cone for good, it was instant peace.

Did you modify your home? Create separate areas for them?

kazann said: "I put Mona in my office where there is no bed to crawl under. I allowed Eli in the room when he wanted in. He does not like to be excluded and is very curious."

If you separated the quadpawds, how long did that last?

Purrkins said: "They were separated by the door until Purrkins was clear 14 days but allowed supervised visits whenever Saxton asked by pawing at he door. We still had a few issues after Purrkins was free it took a good month before things were back to normal for us. We continued the multi cat diffuser and are still using it!!"

What other methods did you try to help everyone adjust?

Jet said: "I separated their food bowl locations (Jerry's on the kitchen table, his on the floor), put litterboxes in multiple locations (now they are both in bathtub in guest bathroom), tried to treat them the same, gave them catnip in same area at same time to hopefully get them comfortable with each other."

Paws120 said: After surgery, Huckleberry earned his own bedroom. He remained crated until after staples were removed, but i let the others visit him after the first several days. After staple removal, i slowly let him have freedom in the closed off room and they played footsies under the door. I re- introduced them one at a time for the first time without him crated and they have done well. Huckleberry is still in his own room and does not have free run of the house yet.

Prepare Children Before Bringing Your Tripawd Home

Kids tend to react to Tripawds in one of two ways, which generally reflect the way that adults around them react. They will either be fascinated and in awe of their amazing capability. Or they will be slightly scared and hesitant to approach. Below are some tips to prepare your human children.

Show them the Tripawds Photo and Video Galleries

Tripawds videos and photo galleries feature many inspiring images of three-legged cats enjoying life. It may even take them a while to notice these kitties are missing a leg!

Next, remind them your new tri-kitty will still have one more leg than they do!

By creating a sense of normalcy around amputation, your kids will be less afraid.

Consider putting a baby onesie on your kitty to hide the incision site.

This may help your kids focus on your cat's strength and adaptability instead of their wounded body.

Finally, spend some time just hanging out together.

Breathe. Relax. Take pictures. Celebrate life. Enjoy the time you have now, and remember that the next phase of your journey will show your kids how much stronger animals are than humans, and how they don't let adversity get in the way of being happy.

More Kids Books about Three-legged Cats

Purr-fectly Lucky (The Purr-fectly Books Book 1) tells the real life story of Meesta the three-legged cat and his strength, spirit, and love. Meesta and his adoptive mom, Kimberly, are on a mission to spread the message that regardless of where your story begins, who you are, or what makes you special and different, everyone deserves a happy ending!

Tripawd Toffee: Adventures of a 3 - legged Cat is an illustrated children's book about the adventures of Tripawd Toffee, a 3-legged cat. He's a beloved pet who's just like other cats, he loves jumping around, climbing on things, and most of all, playing with his friends. Share the journey of the struggles and adventures of a 3 - legged cat, whilst at the same time feeling the love a pet can give you and to teach children about disability.

The Three Legged Cat is the story of a cat named Tom who has only three legs, but dreams of roaming the wide world. Tom's owner, Mrs. Gimble, does not want Tom to be a prowler. She prefers him to be a more sedate cat who gives her no trouble. Mrs. Gimble's brother Cyril, a "rascally, roving swagman" comes to visit wearing a "revolting, moulting Russian Hat" to keep his head warm Tom gets his lifelong dream when Cyril mistakes his hat for the cat!

Pre-Amputation Questions to Ask Your Vet

Easy communication between you and the vet is important for a good recovery. Meet with the surgeon ahead of amputation day and ask questions, such as:

Does my cat have any risks while under anesthesia?

Anesthesia is no longer as risky as it once was. But like any surgery there are risks. We recommend reading the helpful pre-surgery brochure, "Feline Anesthesia," to be more comfortable with anesthesia and to know what to expect before and after surgery day. You'll also want to make sure your veterinarian is following the newest American Association of Feline Practitioner Anesthesia Guidelines, which address a feline's unique anesthesia needs. For your own peace of mind, it's perfectly OK to ask your vet if they are following these guidelines. Also request more details on their plan for making sure your cat emerges from surgery without complications.

What pain management will you prescribe for my cat?

The area of pain management has evolved in the last decade. Gone are the days when vets thought animals needed to feel pain in order to stay quiet and heal. Today, forward thinking vets aim to prevent pain before it occurs. They do this by beginning a pain management protocol a few days prior to surgery and making sure it continues afterward for ten to fourteen days (and sometimes longer).

Unfortunately not enough veterinarians are following the latest pain management guidelines of the American Animal Hospital Association.

Animals can't tell us how they feel. We owe it to them to make sure they're getting the best pain management possible.

Have a pre-surgery discussion with your vet about:
- The type of pain medication your cat will receive
- How and when the medication needs to be given
- The number of days your cat will be taking medications
- What kind of side-effects you may encounter
- and how to care for the incision

> *I would rather have too much medicine and not need it, than be running back for more! Purrkins was on Buprenorphine total of 12 days and the Gaba for 14 days.*
> – PURRKINS MOM, HOLLY

! Please see chapter six for important details about post-amputation pain management options to discuss with your veterinarian.

Will you leave a scapula or stump, or remove the entire area? Why or why not?

The decision to leave any part of the limb depends on if the pet has a limb cancer, the size of the tumor and where it is located. The surgeon's own personal preference also factors into the decision. Dr. Michael Lucroy, an oncologist from Indiana, told us:

> *In our practice, our surgeons always do what is known as a forequarter amputation – that is they take everything from the scapula on down. This is my preference because it is faster for the surgeons, so less anesthesia time for my patients."*
> – DR. MICHAEL LUCROY, DVM MS DIPLOMATE ACVIM

Removing the entire limb is cosmetically appealing to most people and it's also more comfortable. This is known as a "scapulothoracic disarticulation." That's when the entire limb is removed from toes to the scapula (shoulder blade). In a cat or dog, the front leg only has muscles that attach to the chest wall. Those muscles are cut in this type of amputation.

In a rear limb amputation, surgery can be done two different ways. In the first technique, a surgeon cuts the muscles at the mid-thigh, and the femur is cut close to the hop. This leaves a well-padded stump that provides cushion for the Tripawd. In the second, the leg is removed at the hip joint and only the pelvis and surrounding muscles are left.

Front or rear, it's long been though that leaving more residual limb may cause problems. "The muscle surrounding the nub will atrophy and the underlying bone looses its cushion." Dr. Lucroy explained. "If the tumor is in the femur, the entire leg always comes off. If it is in the tibia, then I defer to the surgeons and they do a high mid-shaft amputation. There is a ton of muscle over the bone so usually they do OK," he says.

This approach to amputations is evolving over time. A 2022 paper on <u>Canine Pelvic Limb Amputation</u> states that leaving a partial limb can cause a greater likelihood of muscle atrophy and pressure sores.

Advances in pet prosthetics are encouraging more vets to lean toward partial limb amputations. If you think you want to try a prosthetic limb for your cat, you need to decide before amputation surgery. Prosthetic limbs need a significant bony area to grab onto. If a Tripawd doesn't have the right amount of limb left over after amputation, a prosthetic is never an option.

There is still considerable debate about partial versus full leg amputation. Each method has its pros and cons. Be sure to talk to your vet before surgery to decide on the best method for your cat.

What medications / supplements should be stopped before surgery?

Make a list of all supplements and medications your cat is taking and review them with your vet. Some supplements will thin the blood and should not be taken prior to surgery. These include but may not be limited to:

- Alfalfa
- Chondroitin (Glucosamine is OK)
- Omega-3 supplements (Salmon and Fish Oils)
- Garlic
- MSM
- Probiotics

- Reishi mushrooms
- Turmeric/curcumin
- Vitamin E
- Vitamin C

Will the incision be bandaged? If so, do I need to change it?

The most beneficial use of a bandage is to collect drainage. Bandaging is far more challenging for rear-leg amputees, so most return home without one. If your cat is losing a hind leg, you may see drainage from the incision.

Incision bandaging has changed through the years. When our dog's amputation incision was left unbandaged we were shocked, but the vet reassured us that air drying would help the site heal faster as long as we kept it clean.

Some front-leg amputees leave the hospital with compression bandages, but the bandages often come undone, bunch up, or hide what's going on underneath, like swelling or infection. Bandages applied too tightly can interfere with circulation.

A compression bandage can help reduce the risk of seromas (fluid build-up) in front leg amputees. We haven't noticed a difference in how well Tripawds heal with bandages versus without. Some members reported cases where post-op complications occurred because a compression bandage was applied too tightly. Ask your vet if your cat's bandage is concerning.

How long can I expect the surgery to last?

Your cat's amputation can take anywhere from 45 minutes to over an hour. The time it takes depends on the size of your cat, whether or not a tumor is being removed, and the clinic's case load for the day.

Ask your vet when you can expect an update. If you don't hear from the clinic within that time frame, don't hesitate to call. You're not bugging them, and you won't interrupt the surgery by calling the front desk.

! TIP: Try to schedule surgery for mid-week, when the clinic's case load is lightest. Mondays and weekends are often filled with emergency situations that can take staff away from caring for your cat.

How long will my cat stay in the hospital?

Pet parents are usually shocked to learn that most animals only stay one night in the hospital after amputation surgery. Most are standing within 12 hours and ready to go home within 24 hours.

Your vet won't release your cat until all vital signs are stable. She also needs to stand up and eliminate on her own, as well as show some kind of interest in food.

- Does your schedule allow you to consistently care for your cat when she comes home?
- Are you uncomfortable bringing her home from the hospital so soon after surgery?

If so, don't hesitate to ask your vet to allow your cat to stay an extra night or two. They almost always happily oblige. An extra night in hospital can work well if you need more time to prepare you, your home, family members and schedules.

On Surgery Day: Relax, Breathe, Sleep

On surgery day you'll probably be nervous, emotional and scared. That's OK, it's human. But for your cat's sake, you'll need to hold the tears back until you are alone. The best thing you can do for your cat is project strong, positive energy. Animals mirror our emotions. What we project, they reflect back at us. Do your best to set a hopeful tone. Stay calm and optimistic.

Should You Visit Your Kitty in the Hospital?

Most vets prefer that clients do not visit their pets in the hospital. That's not to spare you the shock of seeing your cat as a Tripawd, but to prevent your cat from getting overly excited because you're there.

Pets become very anxious when they see their humans, only to be confused when they are left behind. As a result, clinic staff has to work hard to calm them down and get them back into recovery mode.

Unless your cat is having issues or refuses to eat, we don't recommend visiting. Yes it's hard to stay away but you both need your rest and once your cat returns, you'll have plenty of time to bond over the next couple of weeks.

If your cat needs to be in the hospital for more than a few

nights, a short visit may be just the thing your Tripawd needs to perk up her appetite and help get her motivated enough to safely return home.

Recommended Reading:
- Extensive reading lists with links to related articles and videos are available in the Premium E-book. **Save $5 OFF with coupon code: BASIC5**
https://tri.pet/tricatbook

CHAPTER 5
Bringing Home Baby

Immediately after the surgery, the pain your cat was experiencing will be gone. Any post-surgery pain will pale in comparison to what she was experiencing before. But, there will be post-surgery challenges. Remember, amputation is a major surgery, and as easy as pets can sometimes make it look, the road to recovery can be long and challenging.

The recovery experience is both similar and different for cats. They are a lot like people when it comes to amputation recovery. For example, some cats won't let you do anything for them because they want to do it all themselves. Others are drama queens, seeking sympathy from everyone around them, whining and crying at every opportunity (especially when the reward is food or affection!). However your cat does in recovery, she will always look to you for guidance. Set the tone and your cat will follow.

How to Stay Pawsitive During Recovery

After surgery, you'll notice that your cat's walk has changed. This may make you sad. It can be bittersweet to see her hopping toward you. Try your best to put those feelings aside, and celebrate that your cat is out of pain, resilient, and coping with amputation far better than any human ever would.

During the first few weeks, do your best not to get discouraged if you think progress is slow. Although it's reassuring to read about other tri-kitty recoveries, don't compare your cat's recovery with others. Remember that recovery times are all different for each cat, and progress is gradual, anywhere from a couple of weeks to a couple of months. Always remember to embrace the little steps along the way.

Your cat will heal at a different pace than other three-legged cats. She's independent and on her own time. Don't force her to do anything she doesn't want to do, but protect her by ensuring she doesn't over-exert herself, for example by allowing her to free roam outside, unsupervised. Make sure she is comfortable, supported and protected, while giving her enough confidence to get back up on her own three feet to take on the world.

What to Ask on Pick-Up Day

When you pick up your cat from the clinic you'll have a million thoughts going through your mind. Before leaving with your new tri-kitty, be sure to ask your vet these important post-amputation questions. That way you'll be prepared for anything that might arise when you get home.

! Review your <u>questions asked before surgery</u>, to ensure you feel confident about the answers you received.

Question #1: What were the last medications given and when?

Ask what pain medication your cat is taking and when you should give her the next dose. Stick to the schedule your vet recommends to keep pain from spiraling out of control. However, sometimes medication schedules need fine-tuning for more consistent relief. Call your vet if you believe medications are wearing off before the next dose is due. Stay ahead of the pain, because when pain gets out of control it's much harder to get it under control.

A journal or spreadsheet to keep track of your cat's medications, quantities and times given can be helpful. You'll find some samples here in the back of the book. Jot down any unusual behavior, just in case you need to discuss it with your vet.

Question #2: When can I restart supplements?

You'll want to know when you can safely restart giving any supplements your cat was taking prior to surgery. If you plan on changing your cat's diet or if she will be undergoing chemotherapy, you may need to wait on supplements during treatment. Many oncologists recommend holding off on new foods and supplements items until all treatments are done.

Question #3: How soon until our follow up visit?

Most cats will have their sutures or staples removed within 10 to 14 days. Generally, that's when the worst of the recovery period is over. But again, if your cat experiences any reactions that concern you, don't hesitate to call your vet before your next visit. A phone call can go a long way toward putting your mind at ease. Don't feel bad about calling the clinic with any questions. They would rather hear from you if you suspect something isn't right, than wait for your call if things suddenly get much worse.

Question #4: What should I do in case of an emergency?

Post-surgery emergencies are rare, but it's always better to be prepared than sorry. Be sure to ask your vet:
- What should I do if I think something is wrong with her?
- Who can I call after hours?
- Where is the closest 24-hour vet clinic?

If you have any concerns about your cat's behavior once she's released, write down the symptoms, when they started and how frequently they occur; then call your vet.

The First Few Days of Recovery

When your cat returns home, always focus on her beautiful face, not her surgery site. Putting on a baby onesie (see Chapter 7) can help.

Your cat should be alert enough to stand and hop on her own by now. She may look tired and a bit confused, but please don't mistake that for depression or anger towards you.

Most times, what humans think is depression in their cat is just the cat's reaction to pain medication. Effective painkillers can induce whining, crying and anti-social behavior. Remember, your cat isn't used to these drugs, and they're probably making her see pink elephants.

Most often, reactions to pain meds is the cause of the change in behavior. Or, your cat could be coping with a condition called Phantom Limb Pain. This occurs when a cat's nervous system hasn't yet realized that the affected leg is actually gone. This painful condition is also common with human amputees.

How to Care for the Amputation Incision

First: Do **NOT** let your cat scratch or lick her stitches!

Post-op Wound Protection is Most Important

Your vet's skillful and expensive work can be destroyed in seconds when a new Tripawd disturbs the incision by licking or chewing. We hate to say it, but leaving the cone of shame on is the best way to ensure that the incision is not harmed. A baby onesie can work in its place, but e-collars are the most effective way to prevent cats from bothering the incision.

Excessive itching or licking can mean that the incision is bothering your cat because it hurts or itches. It can also indicate inadequate pain control. If your cat scratches just once or twice at the incision it could cause an infection so do your best not to let it happen. When you notice your cat obsessing over the wound, let your vet know.

Do not apply any healing ointments like Neosporin or Manuka Honey without discussing it with your vet. If your vet approves, you may want to ask them about a veterinary wound healing spray such as Microcyn Wound Care. This topical spray has no steroids, is non-toxic, cleans wounds and kills bacteria, including MRSA. We've had great success using this for Tripawds Spokesdog Wyatt Ray.

Keep the Incision Clean

Inspect the incision daily to make sure it's clean and dry. This helps to avoid infection and other serious complications like MRSA (methicillin-resistant staphylococcus aureus) a bacterial skin infection that strikes pets (and people) who have weakened immune systems. It's not common, but we do see it here. Although your vet will give you an antibiotic to ward off any infections, do not let your cat outside until you are cleared to do so. You need to give the site time to heal without risking bacteria and dirt getting inside the area.

Check the bandage daily.

Make sure that it doesn't cut off circulation, whether your cat is standing or laying down. A compression bandage should be snug but you should be able to get two fingers under it. Because compression wraps support muscles and swollen tissue, there should be less fluid production.

Despite these precautions, you can expect some bruising and leakage from the area to occur.

Watch for a Seroma.

A post-op seroma is an accumulation of fluid and blood at the surgery site. Think of it like this; all bodies are filled with fluids that move around inside. When a leg is removed, those bodily fluids have nowhere to go. They often puddle up at the area of least resistance; the surgical site. The seroma will become puffy and swollen and may or may not leak. Some veterinarians will attempt to avoid seromas by placing a drain in the area while closing off the incision.

According to Michigan Veterinary Specialists...

> *Seromas may occur at the surgical site. A seroma is an accumulation of fluid in the tissues. The body will usually absorb the fluid, but the fluid is sometimes drained if needed.*

Northern California's Veterinary Surgical Associates say:

> *If the region around the incision becomes progressively more swollen, your pet may have a seroma, which is an accumulation of fluid under the skin This occurs most often with dogs (and cats) that are very active immediately after surgery.*

Seroma fluid is watery in appearance, with pink tint from blood. It should not appear dark, or as 100 percent blood. A seroma is no cause for alarm, but do call your vet if it gets large. You'll want to find out if the area should be drained in the office. Sometimes seromas need to be drained more than once, but often the body reabsorbs the fluid.

Cover your cat's sleeping area with old towels to soak up excessive fluid leakage. A soft absorbent towel with warm soapy water can be used to gently clean up around the incision if it leaks. Contact your vet immediately if you notice any signs of infection such as:

- Cloudy, thick discharge
- Missing staples or loose stitches
- Foul smells coming from the area
- Tissues protruding from the incision

How to Reduce a Seroma

To help seromas dissolve, Tripawd's fairy vet mother, Dr. Pam Wiltzius, suggests using a warm compress at the site.

> *Cold packing is for swelling / inflammation. Hot packing is to help loosen muscles up prior to massage and the heat can also stimulate the body's cells to absorb the extra blood . . . If a seroma is going to burst there is not much you can do to prevent that and the heat can actually help bring the fluid to*

the surface which is what you want. Ideally a vet would have drained the fluid before it burst or put a drain tube in.

- POST-AMPUTATION SIDE EFFECTS

A warm compresses with a warm washcloth (5-10 minutes 2-3 times daily) should help encourage drainage and a compression bandage (changed daily) is also beneficial.

Watch for Unusual Bruising.

Bruising happens as a result of skin, muscles and tissues being cut to remove the leg. The amputation site becomes traumatized by the leg removal, and bruising often happens. If you see this, don't panic – it's usually not as bad as it looks, and also indicates healing is taking place.

The bruises can become an angry, dark purplish color and may get darker a few days after surgery but will fade into a yellow color over the next few weeks. If the bruised area grows in size after a few days, let your vet know.

! TIP: Heat will increase circulation. Ice will reduce swelling. When using ice/heat therapy, always end with ice.

Heat and Ice Therapy to Minimize Bruising and Swelling

If you're not sure when to use heat and ice after amputation or other surgeries, you're not alone. Many people are confused about when to apply heat, how to apply ice and the amount of time to apply it to cats and dogs. Our blog post, Heat and Ice Therapy Tips has everything you need to know to apply it correctly if your cat will allow it. In short:

Ice therapy constricts the blood vessels to stop inflammation and resulting pain. It should be used during the first 72 hours after surgery.

Moist heat therapy encourages healing by increasing blood flow at the incision. It decreases pain too and is also very soothing to your pet. But it should never be used during the first 72 hours after surgery. When 72 hours are up, animal massage therapist Wendy Richardson recommends rotating heat and cold as follows:

- First: Apply heat for 3 minutes. Heat will loosen the fibers and increase blood flow to the area. Always test heat before application.
- Next: Apply cold for 2 minutes. Ice reduces swelling and inflammation. Crushed ice can be used, wrapped in a thin towel for the cold application.

Using the Litter Box

Wondering how your cat will use the litter box on three legs? You're not alone. This is one of the biggest concerns of most new Tripawd parents! But rest assured, cats figure this out quickly. As our vet once said to us, "When they need to go...they'll go!"

Post-op urinating usually happens relatively easily, but sometimes it can take up to a few days for a bowel movement, so don't be alarmed. Many pain medications cause constipation. Most cats won't have a problem with urination, but will not have a bowel movement until anywhere from two to five days after surgery. You can expedite things by adding tiny amounts of MiraLax (polyethylene glycol powder) to her food. The dosage range is anywhere from 1/8 to 1/4 teaspoon given orally twice a day with food. Larger cats may need a heaping tablespoon. Give it at least a day before expecting results.

Make a Tripawd-Friendly Litter Box

Sometimes a cat's litter box poses problems for the new amputee. In <u>this Tripawds Forum Discussion</u>, Sherman's Mom writes:

> *He is doing GREAT, he runs and plays and is thriving...The only issue is when he is in the litter box, he seems to have phantom leg issues and tries to cover up his "business" using his amputated leg. He seems to get frustrated and gets his shoulder closer and closer to the litter trying to move it and cover it up. He sometimes ends up getting litter on his face and his belly, and he seems really frustrated. Then eventually he seems to realizes that leg won't work, and uses his other front leg. It makes me sad to see him struggle, is there some sort of therapy or training I can do with him to help him?*
>
> – <u>SHERMAN'S MOM</u>

The tri-kitty community came through with lots of great ideas for Sherman. We shared them in our Litter Box Tips for New Tripawd Cats post that included helpful suggestions such as:

Have multiple, clean boxes.

Being able to potty in a CLEAN box is extremely important, especially for recovering rear-leg tri-kitties who may have a hard time standing while pottying. Keep multiple boxes and maintain a good scooping schedule to keep the litter as clean as possible.

Use non-clumping litter.

A leaky incision can cause litter to stick to it. If your cat isn't fussy about changing litter, you can minimize the risk by introducing an organic, non-clumping litter before amputation day, like Dr. Elsey's Senior Cat Litter. This litter absorbs urine odor and bacteria on contact, traps it inside the silica crystals, and wicks it away from the cat's body. It won't stick to a cat's long hair either.

Boxes should have two separate entrances and exits.

"Cats, especially limited-mobility cats, really like to have an entrance and a SEPARATE exit path from the litter box," says Feta in her "Litter box Hacks," blog post.

Protect the floor under the box.

Your new tri-kitty's aim may be off while she gets accustomed to being a Tripawd. Make sure your floors are protected by placing old towels, newspapers or pet pottie pads underneath the litter box.

More Helpful Recovery Tips from tri-kitty Members

▶ Tripawds Three Legged Cats Discussion Forum
▶ All 100+ Tripawds Three Legged Cat Blogs
▶ Tripawds News: Top Tips for Tri-kitties

Recommended Reading:

▶ Extensive reading lists with links to related articles and videos are available in the Premium E-book. **Save $5 OFF with coupon code: BASIC5**
https://tri.pet/tricatbook

CHAPTER 6
Pain Management

" He hopped out of his carrier (doing a face plant into the carpet), awkwardly scrambled to the kitchen, and ate some food. All of that made me feel wonderful!
- HENRY BLUE EYES

The Best Way to Manage Post-Amputation Pain

Cats and dogs differ in many ways, but both will do anything they can to hide pain. When your cat comes home from surgery the first few days can be challenging as you try to figure out if your cat has adequate pain control, or not enough. Nearly every new Tripawd parent reports that their cat's behavior during the first few nights after surgery includes rapid breathing, more vocalizing, anxiety, inappetence (refusing to eat) and just acting weird. Some even report a disturbing but common phenomena, walking backwards. Many cats may seem depressed and become constipated, sometimes for up to a week.

It's hard to see our pets going through this, but chances are that most unexpected behavioral changes are often from pain medication side effects. Try to remember that whenever you take a pain pill yourself, you are usually prepared and know what to expect, which helps mitigate any side effects. But your cat, however, has no idea that painkillers can make her feel weird. Talk about being surprised! The resulting behavior is lethargy, confusion and what many consider to be depression. We're not saying that your cat isn't feeling badly, because she is. But that sad look on her face isn't anger or regret over the amputation–animals simply aren't burdened with our human emotions. That's not to say they don't feel pain. Just like us, they do. Which is why it's important to manage the pain well and stay ahead of it.

Stay Ahead of the Pain.

Using pain medications in anticipation of pain is more effective than waiting until the pain already exists. Following the medication schedule your veterinarian prescribes is key to managing pain.

PAIN MANAGEMENT

Don't leave the hospital until you talk with your vet about the medications your cat is being given. Get answers to questions like:

- How often to give the pain medications?
- What to watch for if your cat needs more frequent doses?
- What kind of side effects can happen?
- What happens if you miss a dose?

Pain control is one of the most challenging aspects of amputation recovery. A good conversation with your vet before your cat returns home will help you both sleep better at night.

It is possible to keep dogs (and cats) with amputation nearly pain-free. Not all of it, but most of it. Some of it happens during the surgery, but certainly going home is really important. Cats do hide their pain and if you aren't treating it properly this can lead to some long-term mal-adaptive issues.
– DR. MIKE PETTY
HOW TO HELP YOUR TRIPAWD'S
POST-AMPUTATION RECOVERY PAIN

Don't assume your vet knows everything about pain control. Odds are, if your vet graduated from school back in the 1980s or earlier, most likely they didn't learn pain control procedures as a student. Common thinking back then was that pain is good for animals because it keeps them quiet. If your vet hasn't kept up with the latest pain management guidelines, your cat could suffer unnecessarily.

People I've talked to about amputation (who have gone through it with their pets themselves) have been kind enough to tell me that vets have extremely different approaches when it comes to pain management. Apparently theories have changed over the years, so vets trained in the recent-ish past may not do as much to PREVENT pain as they do to treat the pain once it occurs. This is an issue, because there are things that can be done to prevent some of the pain from ever occurring.
– TRI-KITTY FANG'S STORY: PAIN MANAGEMENT

Veterinary pain management expert <u>Stephen Cital</u>, RVT, SRA, RLAT, VTS- Lab Animal Medicine, agrees. Stephen is a renowned veterinary nurse and educator with a focus on veterinary anesthesia, exotic animal care and education for veterinary nurses. He says during his career he has often seen cats miss out on proper pain relief.

"I think cats have historically gotten the short end of the rope," he told us in our Tripawd Talk Radio Podcast, <u>Managing Amputation Pain in Cats, Before During and After Surgery</u>. "But I think the biggest reason that cats aren't getting the same level of pain management compared to our dog friends is because the practitioner maybe doesn't understand the pharmacology of certain drugs with cats."

Cats are extremely stealth about showing weakness, even more than dogs. Historically, vets have been more focused on treating pain in dogs because they are better at showing when they hurt, and when they feel better. Far more is known about dogs and pain because they're easier to read than cats.

"Cats are so good at hiding their pain and pretty stoic. They don't necessarily look like they're pain," explains Stephen. "But that's not necessarily true. We know that cats and dogs are feeling the same level of pain because they're both mammals and they both have the same nociceptor system. That nociceptor system is that system that is responsible for transmitting pain signals throughout the body into the brain. Cats and dogs have the same thing, we just don't treat it the same because there's a lack of education and lack of understanding on the practitioner side."

But there are some ways that cats do tell us they hurt, which include:
- Less desire to interact with people and animals
- Sleeping in an unusual position or location
- Unusual aggression when approached
- Resisting handling or being picked up.
- Decreased grooming and mat formation OR increased grooming in specific areas
- Stiffness or limping
- Changes in personality
- And perhaps the most surprising pain indicator of all: purring!

"Purring does not necessarily mean that they are happy all the time," explains Stephen. "Even purring can be a sign of discomfort. We know that cats in the wild, they can purr at certain frequencies to actually heal the bone." He goes on to explain that in human medicine, researchers are trying to utilize this "natural technology" and create medical devices that stimulate bone growth by emitting the same frequencies as a cat's purr.

Whether your cat is in amputation recovery or weeks out from surgery, the important thing is to listen to your inner voice when you suspect your cat is hurting. Don't wait until their pain is so bad it's obvious. By then, an animal is probably experiencing horrific pain that no human would tolerate.

When I was rubbing her leg I noticed it felt strange and thick. She wasn't limping or acting like she was in pain...
- MISTY GREY

Know Common Cat Pain Indicators

The Cat Pain Signs Checklist can help translate what your cat is trying to tell you. Take notes, then call your vet asap to discuss what you're seeing. Please ask your vet for a clear action plan for treating the pain. Sometimes all it takes is rest and medication. Other times managing animal pain may require additional support from a certified animal rehabilitation therapist.

If you're not seeing improvement in your cat after following your vet's plan, we urge you to discuss this with them. If the vet seems stumped, ask for a referral to a veterinary pain management specialist who belongs to the International Veterinary Academy of Pain Management. These vets know more than most about animal pain because they specialize in treating it, and they're on the leading edge of pain management studies and treatments. Visit one like Dr. Mike Petty at Arbor Point Clinic in Michigan and your cat soon feel good again.

Common Pain Management Medications for Cats

If you're new to pain management drugs for cats, you'll want to get acquainted now. As we suggested earlier, listen to our Tripawd Talk Radio Podcast "Managing Amputation Pain in Cats, Before During and After Surgery" with feline pain management expert Stephen Cital. In this episode you will learn about feline pain management after surgery, and what kind of drugs you should expect your vet to provide.

Even with great pain medication, sometimes a drug that works great on one cat, may not work so well on the other. All creatures metabolize a bit differently. Many pain management drugs that work well on dogs are given to cats, but sometimes those drugs don't work as effectively across species. Your job during recovery is to watch your cat for signs of discomfort even when she does receive proper pain medications. If one pain medication doesn't help your cat feel better, don't hesitate to call your vet and ask for another. "In general, I would say we have really good options for cats and there's really at this point no excuse to not provide them with appropriate pain management," says Stephen.

Ideally you want your vet to prescribe a combination of medications. "What's nice about mixing different drugs or doing 'polypharmacy' is when you mix different drugs, some of these drugs play really nice together and they can potentiate each other so it makes them work better and we can use them at lower dosages," says Stephen. "This is going to get rid of some of the negative side effects we would see with a big, huge dose of buprenorphine or a big, huge dose of a particular nonsteroidal anti-inflammatory."

The following are the most common pain medications given to cats after amputation surgery.

Non-Steroidal Anti-Inflammatories (NSAIDs)

These drugs reduce mild to moderate painful swelling and inflammation in the body. Care must be used, as the kidney and liver can be affected. And never give your cat a human NSAID, which can be lethal. Veterinary NSAIDs include:

Robenacoxib (also known as Onsior) is approved for short-term, post-surgery recovery in cats. Many feel it is a better, safer option than the controversial Metacam.

"It works a little bit more locally than systemically, which adds to its safety profile," explains Stephen. Robenacoxib has less of a risk for renal, liver and GI problems. And while the official dosage says it can be used for three days without problems, Stephen explains that a recent study shows it can be used up to 28 days without any detrimental effects. "That is one I definitely like to lean on," he says.

Robenacoxib is preferable because <u>Metacam</u> has been shown to cause acute renal failure and death when given to cats on a long-term basis. However, veterinarians do know that Metacam considered safe when given as a one-time, single injection after surgery.

Either NSAID may be injected by your vet after surgery or given to you in oral form to administer to your cat. In all cases, your cat needs to stay hydrated when on this type of medication. "Hydration is going to be super important to keep those kidneys running normally especially when we're giving something like an NSAID," says Stephen.

Opioids

For immediate post surgery and extreme pain, opioids are given. These drugs may be used in combination with a NSAID and may include the following.

<u>Tramadol</u> is often used for mild to moderate pain control but with a bitter taste that cats hate.

<u>Codeine</u> is also used for mild-to-moderate pain relief.

<u>Fentanyl</u> is most commonly applied as a skin patch for severe pain relief that is 75 to 100 times stronger than morphine.

<u>Hydromorphone</u> is a strong, sedating opiate for severe pain that may cause nausea and vomiting.

<u>Buprenorphine</u> (Buprenex) is an injectable, oral or transmucosal drug that <u>should be used with care</u>.

<u>Simbadol</u> is an injectable version of Buprenorphine with high success rates in felines.

<u>Zorbium</u>, newly released in July 2022, is a buprenorphine transdermal solution. It's the first transdermal buprenorphine animal drug intended to control postoperative pain in cats. Your vet can give it to your cat in the hospital, a single application provides pain relief to the cat for four days! It means you'll spend less time medicating your cat.

<u>Buprenorphine</u> is an opioid pain medication that works by acting on pain receptors in the central nervous system. Zorbium is a solution that's applied to the skin at the base of the cat's neck and is rapidly absorbed into the layers of the skin. It provides pain relief within one to two hours following administration and continually releases buprenorphine into the body over a period of days.

Gabapentin (Neurontin) and Amitriptyline both deserve a special mention here, because of the risk of phantom limb pain in new amputees (see Chapter 7 for more information about phantom pain in cats). Currently they're being used in an 'off-label' method by veterinarians, meaning it's legal to prescribe to animals but there are no long-term studies showing its effectiveness for any species other than humans. As a result, your cat's dosage may need adjustment.

Gabapentin for post-amputation nerve pain relief has been commercially available since 1993 but use in animals is relatively new. Its efficacy remains debatable in the veterinary community and many vets still don't routinely prescribe it to new amputees. Some vets just aren't convinced Gabapentin works, and many Tripawds parents still have to advocate for this pain reliever. If you feel your cat is suffering from phantom limb pain, please ask your vet about it.

Amitriptyline is another drug that can help with this problem as well as anxiety. Along those lines, your vet may want to prescribe a similar type of drug known as **Benzodiazepines** (BZs). This class of drugs includes Valium and Midazolam, among others that work well with opioids. When used in combination with an opioid, less of the opioid is needed for pain control. The way they work together is simple, Stephen explains. "If you think of an opioid molecule and it's in the body and then you think about adding a benzodiazepine, the benzodiazepine molecule acts almost like shepherd for that opioid molecule and helps it get to that particular receptor (where) it's supposed to

work better."

Nocita (bupivacaine liposome injectable suspension) is the newest injectible post-surgery pain relief for cats. A time-release version of bupivacaine, Nocita is administered by your veterinarian when closing the incision wound, and lasts for three days afterward. If your vet doesn't offer Zorbium, ask for Nocita.

How to Give Pain Medications to Your Cat

Your cat's recovery depends on good pain management. Purrkins' mom Holly wrote this excellent post about how to give

pain medication to your cat in the Tripawds Discussion Forums:
▶ Administering Medications to Your Cat

Syringing, Pilling, Pill Poppers and Transdermal Gels

Using Syringes: Can you syringe your cat? Yes! We personally prefer the syringe. Syringing is less stressful for our cats. You have to be careful with how you administer liquid medication, administering too fast or improperly could lead to aspiration pneumonia. This is caused when a liquid or foreign substance makes its way into your cat's lungs. It causes the lungs to become inflamed and infected. It's an incredibly dangerous condition, and is considered a veterinary emergency. After you give your cat its medicine if you notice signs of coughing, labored breathing, or a discharge from its nose, go to the vet immediately.

Insert the syringe in the corner of the mouth between the cheek and teeth. Never squirt directly into the back of the cats mouth.

The syringe should be placed at an angle on the side of your cat's mouth. Pause and give your cat the time it needs to swallow the liquid at its own pace. Never just squirt the medicine down their throat.

Giving Pills to Your Cat

It's not impossible to give your cat pills. Here are some techniques that can help. Please always follow up with water or food afterwards.

Tablets: Traditional tablets can be pilled, they can be crushed in a pill crusher or mortar and pestle, mixed with a little liquid to be syringed back up the syringe and then syringed to your cat. Some tablets are slow-release or are in a protective coating to survive stomach acid and become active in the intestine. Crushing or grinding such tablets decreases their effectiveness and should be avoided. Ask your vet first.

Capsules: Capsules can be pilled, or they can be opened and poured out in a bowl and mixed with a little liquid to be syringed back up the syringe and then syringed to your cat.

Another trick to try if the medicine is not bitter is to crush it or open a capsule and put it in some Turkey and Gravy baby food. Ham & Gravy, Chicken & Gravy baby foods work great. Our cats love the turkey and gravy baby food. I give them their supplements in baby food. They lick it right up. But remember baby food is high calories. That can be good after surgery. It also can lead to weight gain quickly if you continue. A small jar is 90 calories.

Pill Pockets: Pill pockets are great if you cat will eat them. Our cats are wise they only get tricked a couple times;) Then the pill pocket is eaten and the pill is still sitting there. In our experience with our cats they are great short term. After surgery you do not want to rely solely on a pill pocket and your cat eating it. Use them but have a back up plan just in case.

Many medications are bitter or unpleasant tasting (including Tramadol). This medicine can make your cat froth at the mouth. It is unpleasant for the cat and for you to watch them run away upset and frothing.

Liquid can mask any unpleasant tasting bitter medicine. First ask the vet if this is okay with the type of medication. I always test a pinhead size taste of medicine to see if it is bitter or awful and what I need to do to make it less awful.

For bitter, gross tasting medicine we use tuna juice or sardine water this masks the bitter taste. Liquid could be tuna juice or sardine water (juices out of the cans).

A lot of times medications can be compounded, Liquid flavored, tabs, treats , melts etc. made into a form that your kitty will not mind taking. Ask the vet prior to surgery, it can help the entire process go smoother.

Transdermal Medications

Transdermal Gels are medications specially formulated to be applied to the skin (usually in the ear). This helps it quickly absorb into the bloodstream, preventing stomach upset. They cost a bit more but are a good alternative if your cat refuses to take certain medications. Ask your vet about this type of medication if your cat is experiencing difficulty taking medications.

Recommended Reading:
▶ Extensive reading lists with links to related articles and videos are available in the Premium E-book. **Save $5 OFF with coupon code: BASIC5**
https://tri.pet/tricatbook

CBD / Cannabis for Cats

! This section is available in the Premium e-book. Get $5 OFF with Coupon Code BASIC5.
https://tri.pet/tricatbook

For more information about cannabis use for pets, find many helpful articles and vet interviews at:
https://tripawds.com/tag/cannabis

CHAPTER 7
Recovery

Prepare Your Home for the New Tripawd

Cats make challenging patients. At first it might seem impossible to follow your vet's instructions to keep your cat subdued enough to heal, but the good news is that many others have managed to do it and you can too. If you have the benefit of time you can make easy, affordable modifications for a recovery-friendly home.

I adopted her with the idea that I would need to place steps and ramps to assist her in safely getting around, but she is more of a daredevil than her four-legged brother. She was the first one to jump from the counter into a cupboard, climb up and fall off the mantle, and launch herself off the upstairs railing to the stairs below. I want her to stay safe but she literally has no concept of self-preservation

I know people say to not worry because cats always land on their feet, but what if they only have three feet to land on? Am I being an overprotective mom?
- DAREDEVIL KITTY, @SKITTLESMOM72

Create a Safe Recovery Room

Cats will want to hide when they return from the clinic. They are exercising a natural feline instinct to protect themselves from predators. Your job is to make sure your cat stays in a small, accessible area of your home, what we call a "Recovery Room." Small confined spaces make it easier to administer medicine, and ensure that she doesn't do too much too soon. Whether you use a dog crate or have an extra room in your home to close off for a while, here are great features of a feline recovery room:
- It should be warm and cozy
- Have a door that you can keep closed
- Small enough so you can easily access your cat, especially during medication time.

RECOVERY

Before your cat comes home you want to do the following:

- **Block off jumping and hiding spaces in the recovery room.** This is especially important if there is a bed in the room. All cats will immediately head for the box springs so don't let that happen! Make all areas of the bed inaccessible by stuffing pillows and comforters underneath. Taking apart the frame and placing the mattress on the floor is often the best idea.
- **Remove any furniture your cat can climb or jump onto.** Block off high perches in the room and around your home where your cat likes to hang out. Many new Tripawd parents are often shocked to see their cat high up on a cabinet when they didn't think they could get up there.
- **Place carpet runners or yoga mats on the floor to help your cat walk without slipping.** Traction is critical for three-legged animals to maneuver on slick surfaces.
- **Add a humidifier to put moisture into the air, especially during winter.** Lack of humidity can dry out your cat's bare, thin cat skin and cause itching at the incision area.

Build a comfy sleeping area

Do you know how your cat prefers to snooze? Does she like being curled up? Sprawled out? Under the blankets or on top? Consider all the ways you've seen your cat slumber and re-create the ultimate lounging area for her.

"Choose a style based on the type of bedding your cat has previously preferred for sleeping," says feline behavior expert Pam Johnson-Bennett in her article Keeping Your Indoor Cat Warm in Winter.

"If your cat likes the warmth of getting completely under your bed covers or likes to be partially hidden when sleeping, then one of the semi-enclosed 'A' frame beds may be a good choice for her. Many cats feel more secure when they can feel their backs leaning up against something so if your cat prefers that but doesn't like to be in a cave-like bed, then one of the donut-shaped beds would work. And, if your cat prefers to sleep all sprawled out then a traditional flat heated bed might be your best option. Pay attention to your cat's preferences and also the position she typically tends to sleep."

Have plenty of blankets and towels available during the first two weeks after surgery. Place them strategically around the room so your cat has many options for sleeping and relaxing.

One of the easiest ways to keep your cat contained within the room is to download the instructions to create a cozy cat carrier. This comes in handy for the post-op follow-up vet visit. Keep a small blanket inside the carrier so your cat has a fast place to hide if she wants.

The following are a few other accessories that can make your cat more comfortable during recovery.

Heated Cat Beds, warming mats and orthopedic cat beds can ease soreness and stiff joints. If you buy a heated cat bed, look for models that only get as warm as a cat's body temperature and have automatic shut-off features when the cat steps away.

Window Perches and a cat tree scratching post tower serve two purposes: giving your cat a comfy, warm play to lay and a view of the outside world. Keep it as low to the ground as possible and make sure your cat has an easy, accessible way to use the perch safely, such as pet stairs.

Gentle Phantom Leg Pain Relief

Finally, a Farabloc EMF-Shield Blanket placed inside sleeping quarters can also help your cat have a better recovery. Farabloc is a non-pharmaceutical phantom limb pain therapy that can alleviate pain in amputees humans and animals. It does this by shielding the body from man-made and environmental electromagnetic fields EMF. Purrkins had a good Farabloc experience, which his mom Holly shares here.

This holistic post-amputation product is made with a lightweight, linen-like fabric infused with a special pattern weave of ultra-thin stainless steel and nylon thread that's designed to shield the body from high frequency electromagnetic fields. Studies show the absence of EMFs may reduce pain and improve recovery.

Farabloc can be used to help alleviate phantom limb pain, or just reduce general post-op pain. So far our Tripawds community canines and felines have given it 3-paws up. We would love to hear from more feline members who give it a try.

Recovery

Introduce Feel Good Pheromones

Few situations in a cat or dog's life are as stressful as amputation surgery, recovery and learning to get around on three legs. It might be tempting to ask your vet for a sedative, but why not try an all-natural anti-anxiety pheromone remedy first, like The Feliway Diffuser. Many Tripawds members like Progo have found pheromone products helpful during stressful times.

"Pheromones are chemical signals which are widely used for animal communication," explains Feliway, the most well-known pheromone product manufacturer. "When emitted by one individual, pheromones are then detected by other individuals from the same species. The messages conveyed by the pheromones affect behavior."

Pheromones come in many forms, such as time-released room scents, sprays and collars. This Feliway video explains how pheromone therapy can make life better for stressed cats:

Pheromone wipes can be used inside your kitty carrier for anxiety relief on the go. Wipe the inside walls so that you can create a safer, comfier retreat for your new Tripawd. She will especially appreciate the soothing pheromones when you take her to the vet to get her stitches out. Pheromone travel spray can take the edge off vet visit rechecks too.

Modify the Litterbox

Cat parents naturally wonder if their new tri-kitty will be able to use the litterbox. Most can do it soon after surgery but a few need extra help. As you already know, most cats are leery of change, so go slow with any litterbox modifications.

> *I am a kitty owner just like you, not all cats are alike, but cats, in general, do not like immediate change! In my opinion, only I would not change the litter when kitty comes home from surgery! Enough has changed! Let's not cause any more stress with a litter change!*
> – LITTERBOX TIPS FOR TRIPAWD CATS

If your cat has challenges using the litterbox, try not to panic. Many cats do at first. You can minimize the odds of any ongoing struggles by following these tri-kitty litterbox tips provided by members, such as:

- Use less litter
- Maintain cleanliness
- Allow time to adjust
- Box edges should be low
- Don't cover the box
- Scoop all waste before they exit

Additional considerations about litterboxes for amputee cats include these important points shared by Feta's mom in her post, <u>Bathrooming Battles and Litterbox Hacks for Tripawds</u>:

- **Pellet litter may be slippery.** Clay or something like wheat or corn litter may be a better choice though note: if there are any wounds or incisions still open, litter may stick to them, so something organic and non-clumping is likely to be your best bet.
- **Make an entrance and a SEPARATE exit path from the litterbox.** To help your Tripawd feel extra comfortable, provide them with more than one way to get in/out of the box.
- **Use floor protectors**, cheap rugs, old towels, disposable potty pads, heavy-duty rubber litter mats, etc. to help contain the mess and save your floors/sanity.

Manufactured low sided boxes can be extra helpful, but you may need to make additional modifications for success. Purrkins' mom Holly did just that, by cutting the sides of a low-sided box even lower.

> *We got a low sided litter box for recovery and it still did not help Purrkins. We ended up cutting the front of our litter box out we used a Dremel tool to do it the plastic was really tough to cut. By cutting it out further Purrkins was able to walk hop in and out easier without so much flopping. It made all the difference for him.*
>
> – <u>HOLLY</u>

Your cat might need extra help covering up her mess. It's not uncommon for a new amputee cat to attempt to cover their mess with the missing limb.

Here's an example of Purrkins using the litter box and trying to cover his business. At 01:31 of this video look carefully to see his body working hard to perform the task.

Old bathroom habits can be hard to break for new Tripawd cats, and some cats may always keep trying to use the missing limb. If your cat doesn't appear to be in pain when attempting to use the missing limb, it's probably nothing to worry about. But if the behavior causes you to worry, talk to your veterinarian and let them know.

Smore also had challenges covering up her litter box mess. Her mom wrote that "She used her litterbox with no problem, but covering her poop did not happen. I did help her with that... We've made a few adjustments for it – namely in pillows and boxes for step downs and a larger litter box." She described Smore's litterbox challenges in her Tripawds blog posts:

▶ Surgery and Immediate Post-Op
▶ Smore and I Are Back

If you find your new tri-kitty is having challenges with the litterbox, be patient and try not to panic. In time and with a little assistance from you, cats usually adapt and figure out a new way to handle these tasks.

Finally, if your Tripawd isn't too strict about her litter preferences, you may want to consider Dr. Elsey's special anti-bacterial cat litter that traps bacteria inside the silica crystals, and wicks it away from the cat's body. It won't stick to your cat's fur and can minimize the chances of incision infection.

Extra Litterbox Mods for Special Needs Amputees

Sometimes a tri-kitty needs even more help than usual. Feta is one such cat who had existing physical issues before her surgery. Amputation temporarily made her a 2.5 legged cat, but she made it through recovery thanks to her human's informative blog post:

▶ Litterbox Mods for Severely Disabled Kitties

It's often a good idea to **have more than one box**.

Being able to **potty in a CLEAN box** is extremely important.

Mats, mats, and more mats! I now have two plastic floor protectors underneath my entire setup, for ultimate floor protection, with puppy pee pads underneath in case of spillage.

"Open" access is critical. Wings and walls are a no-go. It leads to a lot of litter spillage, but it's still better than cleaning up messes directly on the floor.

Prepare Other Cats in the House

Everyone plays a part in a successful amputation recovery, even your other cats. Sometimes things don't go quite a calm as one would like when the patient comes home. "Initially Dazzle was very happy to see Tuxedo," writes Mommatux. But then things got interesting, and turned out better than she had hoped:

> *He loved on him and helped groom him. Once the hard plastic cone of shame went on though, things changed. Dazzle would hiss & whack Tuxedo on the head cone whenever he got near.*
>
> – MORE FROM MOMMATUX

You can minimize the chance of confrontations and anxiety by following the tips shared in this Tripawds Three-legged Cats forum topic:

▶ How to prepare your four-legged kitties for the homecoming and recovery of your new tri-kitty?

The following are more helpful tips suggested by experienced tri-kitty parents.

Create a separate recovery space for the tri-kitty

For more harmony in the home, try a Multicat Pheromone Diffuser. This product uses pheromones to help decrease the frequency and intensity of tension between cats in the home. Start as early as possible, even before surgery.

> *Saxton was Aggressive & curious at first! That is normal cat behavior in our multi household, They come home smelling differently and with cats that is huge! Purrkins was so doped he did not react but as recovery went on they both would react to each other. Purrkins being defensive and Saxton not knowing who that strange smelling animal is.*
>
> – PURRKINS

Separate each cat's feeding stations

Finally, "always consider the cats and their relationship," suggests Mona's mom, <u>Kerren</u>. She took both of her cats' personalities into consideration when deciding how much time the should spend together during the recovery. Some cats are agreeable to being separated, some are not.

> *Mona, although smaller than my male Eli, tends to bonk Eli on his head if she thinks he's getting too close," she explained. "She does not cuddle with him although he would like to snuggle with her. Eli is very tolerant. . . I put Mona in my office where there is no bed to crawl under. I allowed Eli in the room when he wanted in. He does not like to be excluded and is very curious.*
>
> – KERREN

How to Protect the Amputation Incision

The Cone of Shame Matters

The cone of shame is the best way to keep animals from harming the tender surgery site. Period. Yes it sucks to see how miserable your cat is while wearing it. And when your cat howls, screeches and wails to get it off, you might be tempted to remove it for just a second. But for your cat's sake, please don't.

If you want to protect your investment in the surgery, keep the cone on your cat. We've seen animals do terrible things to their incision when the cone comes off too soon, even if only for a minute. "I just looked away for a second," members often say, and in the blink of an eye their cat destroyed sutures, which created another vet bill and sometimes caused infection to set in. Don't let this happen to your tri-kitty.

Below are examples of how some Tripawds members got through the cone phase.

Insist on the Cone

When asked <u>what she would do differently during recovery</u>, Mommatux she says she would have "insisted on a plastic cone of shame from day one instead of one of the softer collars that a very determined cat can easily escape from."

Secure the Cone with Tape

Cats are masters at escaping from the cone of shame. Many people already know this about their cat, and take extra precautions to keep it on during amputation recovery.

> *Tuxedo managed to get out of all the various cone collar types except the rigid plastic one, that had to be both fastened skin tight to his neck and secured to his collar.*
>
> – MORE FROM MOMMATUX

Try a Cone Alternative

If a typical cone of shame doesn't work, try a cone of shame alternative like Emily's people did.

> *Our cat Emily just had bladder surgery in June. She couldn't eat with the hard cone, so we got her the toilet seat cone. She couldn't reach anything with that one. I had to wipe her butt, clean her legs, chest and back with baby wipes for a month. Here's a picture of her wearing the medium size one.*
>
> – CHUY MALONE

Comfy Cone Soft Collars are Another Option

This soft, cone-shaped E-collar is made with foam-backed, padded nylon and adjustable closure. It's similar to what Jill wore during recovery.

"It only took about ten minutes for her to get used to it and I honestly don't even think she knows it's on anymore," her mom Erica said in Jill the Cancer Fighting Kitty's blog.

"These collars are surprisingly well-tolerated by cats," writes Dr. Arnold Plotnick, DVM, in the Catster article, "The Different Types of Elizabethan Collars or E-Collars for Cats".

Cone of Shame Alternatives include:

HiDREAM Cat Cone Waterproof Collar

The HiDREAM Cat Cone is only 4oz, which reduces the discomfort when wearing and does not affect the cat's vision. Your pet can eat, drink and play normally.

RECOVERY

Suitical Cat Recovery Suit

Tia the three-legged cat was the first member to show us the benefits of a well-made and well-fitting cat recovery suit, like the Suitical Recovery Suit.

> *I put the suit back on her today with much more success. She reacted with the classic "freeze and flop" that happens with a Thundershirt on a cat. . . The large size fits better in the torso, but the bottoms were too big. So, I am using the smaller size bottoms and the large top. She no longer freezes and flops over and seems to be mobile in this new configuration. She is happy to have the cone off, I think.*
> – POST OP DAY 7, FIRST DAY OUT

Cute E-collars for Cats

Spread some joy during the days of recovery with fun and effective plush collars, available in various shapes and designs.

VetMedWear Amputation Recovery Suit.

Finally, you might also want to try the custom e-collar alternative tailored specifically for Tripawds. The VetMedWear Amputation Recovery Suit for cats and dogs is the kindest way to keep new amputees from licking and scratching at the incision.

The Only Amputation Recovery Suit for Tripawds! VetMedWear is the only company making custom amputation recovery suits for dogs, and cats of all sizes. Just let them know which leg your pet is missing and they will ship an e-collar alternative made specifically for your new Tripawd.

Soft, stretchy fabric. Made from 95% pure cotton, 5% lycra, breathable, hypoallergenic, and washable fabrics. The form-fitting fabric is specially made to promote mobility.

Anatomically Correct too. The blue suit for males has a urination hole. Before going for a walk, simply open the flap and attach it to the Velcro strip located on the side of the Suit. Using this feature is recommended for middle to larger sized pets, removing the Suit may be an easier process for smaller pets.

The pink Suit has a unique trim at the back to allow females to perform all bodily functions without removing the Suit. It is easy to put on your pet. Just guide your pet's legs into the Suit arm holes. Then use the zipper to secure it.

> *This suit was a game changer for my dog Katie's recovery. I ordered the suit and received it before she was released from the hospital so she had it on at discharge. The suit prevented her from licking or scratching at her stitches and was a lightweight material so comfortable even in the NJ heat wave. Katie was able to go to the bathroom without taking it off. I removed it a few times for washing and would highly recommend line dry to prevent shrinking."*
> – KAREN SUTTON

Sew a DIY Baby Onesie Cat Suit

Handy with a needle and thread? You may be able to modify a baby onesie (also known as a "Baby Grow" in the UK) to help your cat recover without a cone.

Jill was the first tri-kitty to introduce us to the concept and Purrkins took it to a whole new crafty level in this excellent instructional post:

▶ DIY Baby Onesie / T-Shirts Cone of Same Alternative

> *Fair warning; these stretch like crazy! Sewing and cutting and writing may not be purrfect. I promise your kitty doesn't care & will be happy they are not in a cone!*
> – HOLLY

The First Weeks After Amputation

Common Post-Op Pain Problems

Many people believe that losing a front leg is harder on the body since animals carry more weight in the front than the rear. And while it's not easy to propel forward on one front leg, the reality is that both front and rear leg Tripawds each have their own unique challenges that can lead to pain, such as:

Front Leg Tripawds:

▶ Put more stress on the front wrist carpal joint
▶ Have a harder time holding objects such as toys and food.

- Find going downhill is treacherous since they carry more weight in front.

Rear Leg Tripawds:
- Lack the propulsion needed to run uphill.
- Can't scratch the front end of their body, such as the neck, ears, chin, etc.
- Lag on going up stairs because all their jumping ability is in the rear legs. One less rear leg makes it harder.
- Often exhibit a "Backwards Walk" after amputation

Whether your cat lost a front or rear leg, recovery should go smoothly. But sometimes pet parents find a few unexpected challenges, which we will spotlight here in order to prepare you for the off chance that they happen to your cat.

The Challenge of Phantom Leg Pain

Tripawd cats, dogs and humans amputees often report the same post-amputation surgery syndrome known as "phantom pains." This condition is the brain's way of telling the body "Hey? Where'd that leg go?!" when it sends a signal to move the missing limb. The nerve is trying to control a limb that doesn't exist. It's a sudden, frightening occurrence that we're seldom prepared for. Tripawd cats with phantom limb pain will suddenly yelp, cry out, jump up or constantly lick the spot where their leg used to be.

> *...every now and then his little stump seems to rear up, almost like he is bucking like a horse, and he ends up rolling onto his side and seems unable to get up. Sometimes he will cry out and I'm not sure if that is pain related or panic. I find that if I talk to him gently and lay my hand on him he stays put and after about 30 seconds he either lies down and relaxes or can get up and move on.*
> – TRACIE121
> <u>CAT DISPLAYING STRANGE BEHAVIOUR AFTER AMPUTATION</u>

If your cat suddenly jumps, cries out, twitches, has muscle spasms and compulsively licks where her leg was, chances are she is experiencing Phantom Leg Pain. It can set in weeks after surgery and last as long as a month, sometimes longer.

> *My kitty did the same and it does pass. It was like a panic attack for her and very scary for me. She'd flip and couldn't seem to catch her balance.*
>
> – NYLAROSE

In this Tripawds News story with pet pain expert Dr. Robin Downing, she tells a story about a dog she treated for phantom pain. The same information is applicable to cats.

> *When there is damage to the nervous system, damage to a nerve and then that nerve tries to regenerate itself. That's the genesis of the phantom limb phenomenon."*
>
> – DR. ROBIN DOWNING, PET PAIN EXPERT

Symptoms of a phantom leg pain condition:

- Limping or dragging a limb
- Shaking or twitching of the skin
- Chewing on the affected area
- Muscle wasting atrophy
- Crying out vocalizing
- Decreased appetite
- Urinating and defecating inappropriately incontinence

Sometimes symptoms will appear much later after recovery, which is exactly what happened to Purrkins. Holly explains in great detail with her blog post about phantom limb pain symptoms and what she did to alleviate them.

> *Dr. Matt was surprised Purrkins was having phantom limb episodes this far out, but he said it could come about at any time. We do believe acupuncture will help it has always done wonders for Purrkins we will just have to get the how often dialed in better we were at every three months as a tune-up. We discussed EMF's Electro Magnetic Fields like a smart meter, wifi routers, laptop, cell phones, microwaves, etc. Post's Jerry has done on the Farabloc go into further detail & a PODCAST: All About Electro Magnetic Frequencies and Tripawd Amputees*

We discussed this because the electric company installed a new smart meter on the house and this does correlate with when Purrkins started having these episodes. Purrkins will be a year and a half post amp next week, and the phantom limb episodes just started happening!
– PURRKINS PHANTOM LIMB PAIN

Phantom pains are common and treatable with rehabilitation therapy that includes modalities like acupuncture and massage. But just because your cat shows common phantom pain symptoms, it doesn't necessarily mean she has phantom leg pain. These two other types of pain often get confused with phantom limb pain.

Hyperalgesia

Treatment for this type of pain differs from how phantom pain is treated. Veterinary pain management expert Dr. Mike Petty describes hyperalgesia as:

Hyperalgesia means that when a painful stimulus is applied to a nerve, the pain that is felt by the dog (or cat) is much greater than what would be expected by the stimulus. For example, we all probably have stubbed a toe or slammed a finger in something. Of course it hurts at the time of the injury, but in many cases, just a small bump of the same area at a later time, often within an hour or two, causes as much if not more pain than the original injury. This is hyperalgesia or "wind-up" pain.
– DR. MIKE PETTY

According to this Veterinary Times article, "Managing Chronic Pain In Cats: Therapy Methods for Chronic Cases," aggressive and fast treatment is required for hyperalgesia.

Aggressive, multimodal treatment may be required for several months before the neuropathic pain component is sufficiently controlled to allow normal petting, grooming and/ or complementary therapies, such as acupuncture...
– GEORGINA BEAUMONT

Myofascial Pain Syndrome (MPS)

Myofascial pain syndrome is another type of pain that affects amputee pets. The condition is basically tight, knotted muscles typically caused by a Tripawd's new stance and gait. Osteoarthritis, overuse and repetitive motion can also contribute. MPS doesn't necessarily happen in the affected limbs, but can occur in other parts of the body like the shoulders and spine. When it gets bad enough, an animal's normal movement becomes restricted and painful.

According to the Animal Pain Management Center in Buffalo, New York, "the most effective treatment for myofascial disease and its pain is deep dry needling. Multimodal pain medication and active PRT is required to compliment needle based therapy and complete the patient's recovery. Low level laser therapy, massage and hands on therapy can improve discomfort. Therapeutic exercise, both land based and aquatic, can help maintain a more function, less painful state."

Troubleshooting post amputation pain in animals is tricky.

If your cat is experiencing these issues, don't hesitate to start looking for a pain management specialist. Many general practice vets just don't see enough post-amputation pain situations. Whatever you do, don't panic, use soothing words and tones to help your cat through any episodes, and reach out to an expert as soon as possible. A vet skilled in the latest pain relief modalities can create a plan using tools ranging from pharmaceutical pain control to acupuncture that will help treat and eliminate the condition over time.

Another Common Situation: The "Backwards Walk"

One unusual issue that sets Tripawd cats apart from dogs is "The Backwards Walk." This is when a new Tripawd cat will literally start walking or scooching backwards for no apparent reason. They often flop and squirm on the floor too.

This behavior can come on suddenly usually right after coming home from surgery and it looks quite scary. No wonder their parents are so distressed when it happens! We have never seen this happen with our canine Tripawds members. Plus, it only seems to happen with rear-leg Tripawd cats for some reason.

> *My concern is that just days after surgery Darwin would have these episodes of walking backwards. He'd lift his stump in the air, sometimes cry out and seemed disoriented for a moment or two. Then he'd recover and all was well. These episodes increased for a time then almost went away completely.*
> – CAT POST-AMPUTATION STRANGE BEHAVIOR

Most vets are usually at a loss about what causes it and how to stop the backwards walk. They theorize that the muscles are having spasms, but no clear causes have been pinpointed. Vets will usually prescribe the nerve-calming drug Gabapentin to see if it helps, and take a 'wait and see' attitude. Most Tripawds members report that the walk eventually goes away but oftentimes we don't hear back from members with updates about their cat, so we never truly know.

If your cat experiences the backward walk issue, keep calm.

Remember it's not the first time this has ever happened. Other members have been through it, and this behavior is more common than most vets realize. The walk usually goes away on its own but if you are not seeing progress, get a second opinion from a good veterinary pain management expert who can assess your cat.

> *I'm so thankful to have found this thread. I'm feeling so stressed and scared for my cat Marcel. I really hope some of you like Tracie121 are still here to offer advice. My Marcel is having these same episodes! His can be very violent. He had a rear amputation 6 weeks ago. About 3 weeks ago after a second surgery to remove infection he started this backwards jolting, walking. He actually flips up, falls all over the place and looks like he could break his neck sometimes. The vets have nothing to offer me! Nothing! I'm so frustrated and feel so alone.*
> – CAT DISPLAYING STRANGE BEHAVIOR AFTER AMPUTATION

You can always get a second opinion from a veterinary pain management expert who can help your cat. Consult the International Academy of Veterinary Pain Management Directory.

Another good resource is <u>AAHA-accredited veterinary practices</u> because they often have veterinarians who at the very least are practicing the most modern pain control methods. Many AAHA clinics also have Certified Veterinary Pain Practitioners on site. You'll know them when you see the "CVPP" initials after their name.

Helping Your Cat with Stairs and Climbing

Whether three-legged or four, cats seem like they can handle any kind of landing or other acrobatics. Or can they? Apparently the success of their stunt depends on many factors.

For example, cats who repeatedly jump from high perches throughout the course of their lives are subject to joint injuries and bone fractures. Dr. Eva Evans, a veterinarian and writer for the <u>Pets Best Pet Insurance blog</u>, explains that cats who fall from higher perches actually have a greater chance of landing on their feet than a cat who falls from a couch or kitchen table.

When cats fall from just a few feet, they often don't have time to fully rotate and they may land on their sides, back or head causing more serious injuries."
– DR. EVA EVANS DVM

A cat's weight also plays an important role.

"Cats who are overweight, uncoordinated or arthritic may not be able to move quickly enough to right themselves, even if falling from a height of 4 or 5 feet. And if cats don't have time to fully rotate, they may land on their side, back or head, sustaining serious injuries," explains this Cat Health article in the <u>Diamond Pet Foods blog</u>.

We lost a 4 legged cat from a fall off our kitchen table. Compound fracture, he was not a candidate for surgery. So going into this with Purrkins front leg amp we were doing the better safe then sorry route. I will always suggest steps to any 3 legged animal & four as they age.
– PURRKINS

Protecting your cat's remaining legs is critical. Always be on the lookout for ways in which your Tripawd is at risk of injury in and around your home and yard. Things that your cat may have done safely and naturally before, may be hazardous now.

Although you usually can't prevent your cat from doing things like climbing and jumping, there are many things you can do to lessen the odds of an injury.

- Keep your cat indoors.
- Build a Tripawd-safe Catio.
- Block off the tops of cabinets and other high perches where cats climb.
- Use pet stairs and other objects that offer safe climbing and descending opportunities
- Add carpet treads on stairs
- Put rug runners down on hallways and popular walking paths
- Install a Tripawd-friendly cat tree – something that isn't too high or too challenging.

What I have done for Rusty is put cat stairs in the areas that I know he's going to try to jump to anyway. I have foam tiles around my house as well now for those less than graceful landings.
– RUSTY THE BUNNYMAN

I didn't move any of use favorite spots but added stairs for him to get up and down safely. Stairs to our bed to the sofa to his window seats. We rearranged furniture and moved things closer together. Added some rugs & rug runners for traction.
– PURRKINS

Entertainment Ideas for the Confined Tripawd Cat
Keep Your Cat Busy

During your cat's recovery period, chances are good that she will grow bored with confinement. To prevent boredom (which often leads to chewing at the incision site) you can help her burn off energy by introducing her to interactive brain games.

Food puzzles for cats make great therapy. They stimulate your cat's mind, encouraging fitness and ensuring emotional well-being. Science backs this up. A group of feline behaviorists have

recently documented food puzzles for cats' many benefits.
- Help cats get fit and lose weight.
- Exercise a cat's natural hunting instinct.
- May also reduce behavioral and mental health problems created by indoor confinement.

"Benefits we have observed include weight loss, decreased aggression toward humans and other cats, reduced anxiety and fear, cessation of attention-seeking behaviors and resolution of litter box avoidance."
– FOOD PUZZLES FOR CATS: FEEDING FOR PHYSICAL AND EMOTIONAL WELL-BEING

The report was published in the Journal of Feline Medicine and Surgery. Download the report here to learn about the benefits of food puzzles and how to teach your cat to enjoy them!

Make Your Own DIY Food Puzzles for Cats

In this Modern Cat article, you can learn how to make food puzzles with things you probably already have at home, like:
- An empty plastic water bottle
- Paper towel rolls
- Egg cartons
- Ice cube trays
- Muffin Tins

Hope for the Best, Prepare for the Worst

Recovery isn't always difficult. Most cats handle it pretty well considering that amputation is such a major surgery. But despite your best efforts, sometimes recovery poses a very difficult challenge.

You'll notice a few members have provided good details of their recovery experiences. For example, you'll see that Tibby had a typical amputation recovery journey for a cat, which you can read about at Tibby's Road to Recovery.

She slept A LOT during that first week after the operation. Tibby would naturally be a bit more active at night. On the second week, we started reducing her Buprenex from three to two times a day, and her alertness increased.
– TIBBY

Not all recoveries go according to plan. Sometimes despite your best efforts, things can turn out differently than you'd hoped. Raven's recovery is a perfect example:

> *Discharge instructions placed a heavy emphasis on keeping her calm/inactive. If I let her walk around the room, even if supervised, she is all over the place trying to scheme hiding places, launch onto chairs, objects, etc.*
>
> *She wants to lick the wound and I'm not sure anything is going to stop her short of a colonial-style head & arm stock. She's gotten out of a soft cone once already vet applied. She is also very adept at reversing the orientation of the soft hood like a blown-out umbrella into a 360 degree bib. Most distressingly, she is so darned flexible she is able to lick a portion of her wound with the collar oriented exactly the way it was intended! Now I'm staring at the cat recovery suit I bought her. It now seems laughable.*
> – RAVEN'S PEOPLE

In the end they found some creative solutions to manage her recovery, which you may want to try if your cat is having a hard time.

> *During the first few days after surgery they kept her in a large dog crate to limit her movements. When she wouldn't put up with the crate, they turned their bedroom into 'a padded cell.' Everything but a mattress and a cat carrier with a blanket was removed. Raven took to her accommodations enough to continue healing on schedule.*
> – RAVEN'S PEOPLE

Not all Tripawd Recoveries are Smooth, But Don't Give Up Hope!

You may have to come up with alternative ways of feeding and caring for your cat during recovery, but rest assured that in a few weeks, your cat will most likely find a "new normal" way of life that makes her happy. Tuxedo's story is a perfect example:

> *After three weeks, all bandages & the cone were removed. No more continual vet trips. The open wound has closed. Yes, it has resulted in a nasty looking scar, but my house is no longer a war zone. No more cone and the two cats are now best buddies. With them even sleeping together again.*
> – @MOMMATUX

Animals are far more resilient than we ever give them credit for, until we watch them recover from amputation surgery. Learn to adapt as well as she does, and you probably won't have any regrets about your decision to amputate.

Recommended Reading:
- Extensive reading lists with links to related articles and videos are available in the Premium E-book. **Save $5 OFF with coupon code: BASIC5**
  https://tri.pet/tricatbook

RECOVERY

CHAPTER 8
Helpful Gear for the Tripawd Cat

Amputee cats are relatively low maintenance, but a few things can make your cat's life easier. The Tripawds Gear Shop is your source to find them.

We only resell products that we believe work well for three-legged dogs and cats. While there are a number of harnesses, boots, beds and other gear available for dogs, unfortunately fewer options exist for three-legged cats. Maybe it's because they don't really need these items as much as dogs do. But each day new and interesting products come across our radar that may help improve your Tripawd's quality of life. The Tripawds Gear blog is where you can learn about them.

We haven't yet found any pet gear that's designed specifically for Tripawd animals – yet! But the assistive devices mentioned and reviewed at gear.tripawds.com are there because members have shared their good product experiences with the community in the Tripawds Blogs and Discussion Forums.

Shopping for Your New Tripawd

If you purchase products to make your tri-kitty's life easier, we recommend introducing these items before surgery. This can make the post-op healing phase much easier for your cat. Please know that shopping at Tripawds helps maintain the many free resources available.

There are many items that can help make life easier for you and your cat. We hope you consider reading our reviews and shopping through our links. The small commissions earned help keep your Tripawds community online. The following are some top recommendations from Tripawds members who have tested the products with their own tri-kitties. You will find more feedback from others by searching the blogs and forums. Thank you for your support!

- The Tripawds Recovery Shopping List
- Tripawds Gear Shop: Cat Products

The Best Cat Harness for a Tripawd

The canine support harnesses we recommend such as the Ruffwear Flagline are helpful for assisting dogs in and out of vehicles, and up and down stairs. But as far as we know Tripawd cats don't really need that level of assistance in everyday life. There is one harness, however, that you may find helpful if your cat is used to walking on leash.

The Kitty Holster

We have never found a good harness for Tri-kitties, until now. The Kitty Holster appears to be the best harness for three legged cats whether they are missing a front or rear leg.

When Purrkins and his mom Holly told us about the Kitty Holster cat harness we knew it was going to be good. You see Purrkins is a front-leg cat amputee, and cats or dogs missing a front leg tend to have more challenges finding a good harness that works for their body type.

Purrkins convinced us it was a good one when we saw this video of him walking with the Kitty Holster. He loves getting outside with it on, can you tell?

Right away we knew that if this device works well on Purrkins, it can work on most cats whether they're missing a front or rear leg. Based on its Amazon reviews, many quadpawd cat parents love the Kitty Holster Harness.

Kitty Holster Harness Features include:
- Ultra-lightweight 100% breathable, washable cotton. Includes un-dyed cotton lining that's gentle on cat fur. Also inhibits irritation on delicate skin.
- Easy for cats to wear. Less stressful to your cat and easy for you to put on/take off your cat
- Zero nylon, thin straps or plastic clips which can cause uncomfortable pressure points and skin abrasion
- Many attractive seasonal colors and patterns.

The Amazon reviews for the Kitty Holster Harness are outstanding. Most people say it works great for their cat. Keep in mind that it won't "support" legs or torso the way humans expect from something like an Ace bandage. What it does is act like a safety tool that gets your Tripawd cat outside into fresh air again, safely.

HOW TO HELP YOUR THREE LEGGED CAT

If you decide to buy a Kitty Holster on Amazon for your Tripawd, please let us know how it works for your three-legged feline hero by <u>leaving a review here</u> to help others.

Tri-kitty Traction Tricks

One of the best things you can do for your three-legged kitty is to improve traction on any slick surfaces throughout your house. Nonslip carpet runners and stair treads are best to help prevent injury from falls.

- Hallway runners, rubber-backed throw rugs and <u>stair traction decals</u> can help your kitty feel more confident on three legs and also help avoid any accidental spills.
- Keep fur trimmed between pawpads
- Use carpet runners, foam tiles, or paw wax.

Many of the <u>Tripawd Traction Tips</u> we recommend for dogs should also work well for three-legged cats.

Kitty Scratchers

When it comes to scratching an itch, rear leg amputees have it much worse than front-leg Tripawds. They will try to "air scratch" with the invisible leg, causing their stump to twitch, flail and scare the heck out of parents!

Since you can't always be there to scratch that itch for them, you may want to consider trying this <u>Cat Scratcher Arch.</u>

So ever since Rocky lost his back leg I've seen him so many times tilt his head and see his stump start twitching because he is trying to scratch his ear, of course I always scratch it for him but I felt bad knowing if no one was around to scratch he'd be stuck with a itchy ear. I saw this <u>Purrfect Arch</u>...so I figured what the heck let's try it out.

Got it set up and Rocky was a little hesitant at first but pretty soon he was in love with it. I think he rolled around, rubbed his face, bit at it and played with it for almost 30 minutes. So the reason I am sharing this is just in case any other tripawd kitty parents have the same issue with the itchy ears going unscratched. This is purrfect for your little tripawd kitty!

I know these can be easily made out of board and bottle cleaners as well but...you'll be spending about the same, maybe a little more and all you have to do is pop the end of the scratchers into the board and its ready to go!
– KIM W.

▸ Read more Amazon reviews for cat arch self-grooming scratcher toys: https://amzn.to/3It7EOj

Window Perches and Cat Trees

Can three-legged cats climb? Of course! The only problem is that cats have all of their jumping power in the rear legs. When one leg gets amputated, they lose half of their ability to jump and climb. But that doesn't mean they won't try. Tripawd cats are especially determined to get back to vertical fun. It's up to their hoomans to make it as safe as possible. These Tripawd cat tree ideas show how to choose good ones for safe, happy, vertical adventures.

" *I got Jet a few months after his amp, so he was already used to life on three legs . . . once he felt confident that he could jump up somewhere, then he'd do it. I don't recall him wiping out. But it did make me nervous."*
– JET'S DAD

Orthopedic Cat Bedding

During the first few weeks after surgery, your Tripawd's incision will probably leak. Save yourself from excessive laundry, by keeping your Tripawd's bed covered with old towels or blankets that can be quickly removed and easily washed.

Many pawrents wonder if their Tripawd will need a special orthopedic bed to lay on after surgery. It doesn't necessarily need to be orthopedic but you do want a quality, firm (non-lumpy) mattress that's easy for your Tripawd to walk on, and turn herself around when trying to get comfortable. Your Tripawd should easily be able to stand up on a firm orthopedic cat bed without struggling. Other features available in cat beds like the Snoozer Orthopedic Luxury Microsuede Cozy Cave Pet Bed are nice, but they're not always necessary for your cat to have a great life after amputation.

- Microsuede exterior, Sherpa interior
- Machine-washable cover, 3" orthopedic foam
- Topped with 2" layer of polyester batting for added cushion and comfort
- Extra deep sleep surface
- Rust-proof brass zipper
- Available in a variety of fabric options

PetFusion Orthopedic Pet Beds

The solid 2.5 inch memory foam in PetFusion orthopedic memory foam bed provides an ultra premium base for superior overall comfort, reduced joint pain (arthritis) and improved health, mobility, & energy. Comforts as a calming cat bed for Tri-kitties who suffer from anxiety.

- PetFusion Ultimate Dog Or Cat Bed

What About Wheelchairs?

Many people think a new animal amputee needs a wheelchair. The truth is, most Tripawds don't need one after surgery. They might later on in life as arthritis or other unexpected conditions set in. A wheelchair can enhance a dog's quality of life, but as of now we haven't had any feline Tripawds members mention the use of a wheel chair, although this assistive device does exist for cats.

For example, Yoda the Wheelchair Cat received worldwide attention when he got his wheels. And the renowned animal wheelchair manufacturer Eddie's Wheels says they do make wheelchairs for cats in their blog post "Yes, Disabled Cats Do Use Wheelchairs".

> *We have collaborated with cat owners to successfully fit disabled cats in carts. Cats ARE cats - not dogs - and their first instinct when placed into any device is to try to climb out of it. You have to use some cat psychology when introducing wheels to a kitty.*
> – EDDIE'S WHEELS

Wheelchair Tips for Cats

Cats who are used to wearing harnesses may adapt much quicker to a wheelchair. But even one who hasn't worn a harness before can get trained for wheels by working with experts. If you think your cat can benefit from wheels, please keep the following tips in mind.

"A cart is not ever detrimental to the patient's health and fitness," says animal rehabilitation expert Amy Kramer PT, DPT, CCRT in the Tripawds News blog post: <u>When and How a Wheelchair Can Help a Dog</u>. She explains that it "should only be needed if they are showing other signs of difficulty with gait." Kramer informs us that do-it-yourself homemade wheelchairs can actually cause more harm than good by putting an animal at risk of further injury.

DIY carts can cause more harm than good.

Please don't make your own cat wheelchair. This is because wheelchairs need a perfect fit and only those professionals trained in animal physiology and wheelchair design have the knowledge to fit a cart that's just right for your cat's body. Making one without their guidance can create more problems for your cat.

Regardless of whether or not a Tripawd is ready for a wheel chair, says Kramer, "All amputee pet owners should understand their pet's limitations due to being an amputee, as well as have a home exercise and stretching program designed for their pet."

> ❗ Please, don't put your cat in a cart until you consult with a veterinary rehabilitation therapy expert.

If after extensive pain management and rehabilitation efforts your cat is still having mobility issues, a cart *might* be necessary for a better quality of life.

How to Keep Your Tripawd Safe in the Great Outdoors

The indoor cats versus outdoor cats debate is a touchy one, but we can't ignore that hot button issue here in the Tripawds Nation. That's because nearly every day another new member joins after their cat lost a leg by getting hit by a car, snared in a trap or enduring an unknown horrific accident or abuse that happened while they were out in the neighborhood.

We've seen so many traumatic causes of cat amputations, and feel that all domestic cats, but especially Tripawd ones,

HOW TO HELP YOUR THREE LEGGED CAT

are overall better off when kept indoors. But in the end, only you know what's best for your cat. The excellent International Cat Care blog post "Indoor Versus Outdoor Cats" offers some suggestions to help you decide what to do:

> *Weighing up the pros and cons will help you decide what is best for your cat. It is easier to opt for an indoor only cat right from the start than to convert an outdoor cat successfully into an indoor one. The benefits of keeping the cat away from possible dangers outdoors have to be weighed against the effects on the cat's behaviour.*
> – INDOORS VERSUS OUTDOORS CATS

If you're debating about whether or not to allow your cat to continue going outside after recovery, we hope you'll consider these stories of two Tripawds cat members.

Fang was an outdoor cat before losing his leg, and after.

This tri-kitty hero got the best care a cat can ask for. He was a fortunate cat who lived well into his late teens. His mamma wouldn't change his outdoor life for anything:

> *...maybe I'm against the grain here, but I think that indoor-only life for some cats is so limiting to their happiness that it could be considered almost sort-of cruel. Some don't care, but some really do. I would never limit Fang that way – I just know that it's what he needs.*
> – FANG'S THIRD AMPUVERSARY

Misty Grey Wasn't as Lucky.

> *Two weeks ago yesterday I was sitting by the sliding glass door keeping an eye on Misty while she took her ease outside in the back yard – something we do often, since she cannot be a true in-and-out cat any more. One minute I saw her snoozing there and was talking with my mom and then I looked out the window again and she was gone. I went all around the neighborhood calling her and shaking her bag of treats, but she was nowhere to be found.*
> – MISTY IS MISSING

Sadly, this beloved tri-kitty never returned home to live life on three legs. If your cat has always lived outdoors, please think about how you can offer them the best of the outdoors, while remaining safe from harm.

After all the time, money and emotional energy you've invested in your cat's journey on three legs, why risk anything bad happening? As Dr. Karen Becker says in her article "Brings Out Kitty's Best, Gives Her the Time of Her Life and Boosts Your Special Bond" your outdoor cat can still enjoy the grass, trees, sky and sun beams, but in a more controlled, safe way.

For instance, the Kitty Holster harness previously mentioned is one way you can both get outside and enjoy some fresh air while strengthening your bond. Think your cat won't agree to leash walking? Try these cat leash walking tips from Adventure Cats.

> *Most cats can be trained to walk on a leash, but certain feline personalities are more accepting of new experiences like donning a harness and walking outdoors. The best time to introduce your cat to a harness is as a kitten because he'll be naturally more accepting of it; however, older cats can also learn to walk on a leash if you're patient and make leash training a positive experience.*
> – ADVENTURE CATS

A Catio Provides Safe Outdoor Experience

Perhaps the best way to ensure your Tripawd lives to a ripe old age is to build a Catio enclosure.

"Providing your indoor cat the opportunity to experience the outdoors safely provides both physical and mental stimulation without the risks of free roaming. It also gives her an opportunity for beneficial grounding," says Dr. Marty Becker.

When you're ready to make the investment, you can purchase a pre-designed kit from Catio Spaces. These large enclosures are not a cage, they are stimulating outdoor play areas for cats and their humans. They range from basic to luxurious and everything in-between!

▶ Pre-made designs exist for everything from simple window boxes to large, elaborate fenced enclosures for big yards.

- Catios are the best and only ways to keep your cat safe from predators and other terrible things that await beyond your front door.

These wood-framed, escape-proof enclosures with perches and lounge spaces help solve the indoor/outdoor dilemma faced by cat parents. Catios provide a safe outdoor environment and peace of mind. Birds and wildlife love them too, since over 2.4 billion birds are killed each year by free roaming cats in the U.S. Yikes!

! Shop **CatioSpaces.com** and use the promo code: TRICATIO. 10 % of the sale supports the Tripawds community!

Top 3 Benefits of Catios

1. Protects cats from accidents, predators, poisons, diseases from other animals or getting lost

2. Provides a healthy lifestyle with the enrichment of fresh air, exercise, sunbathing and bird watching

3. Reduces indoor multi-cat issues by adding more territory and stimulation

If you're stuck paying off high vet bills, there are many affordable ways to keep your outdoor Tripawd cat safe, like these temporary outdoor enclosures for cats on Amazon.

When your budget allows, you can get started building your own amazing DIY Catio designed by CatioSpaces.com!

Recommended Reading:
- Extensive reading lists with links to related articles and videos are available in the Premium E-book. **Save $5 OFF with coupon code: BASIC5**
https://tri.pet/tricatbook

CHAPTER 9
Rehabilitation and Continuing Care

How to Get Your Tripawd Eating Again

Many new amputee cats will have a weak appetite after surgery. That's totally normal and usually the result of medication and the sudden change in circumstances. If your tri-kitty doesn't want to eat, don't panic. You can do a few things to boost appetite, from adding food toppers to making a liquid gruel diet to syringe feeding. Here are some tips to get your cat eating again.

Have More Cuddle Sessions

Helping your cat eat again may be as simple as snuggling on the couch. "Some cats simply need to be held more," writes a VetInfo.com author in the helpful article "[Choosing a Cat Appetite Stimulant](#)". Your touch can give calming reassurance to your cat at a time when she feels vulnerable, and needs your presence the most. Pick her up and caress her throughout the day, show your affection and soothe her with gentle strokes at meal times so she can let down her guard and enjoy her meal. You can also do a few more things to encourage your cat to eat.

Serve a warm meal.

Who doesn't like a warm meal? Your cat may enjoy one too. Some people say don't put cat food in the microwave, others feel it's perfectly OK to heat it for 10 seconds or so. If you don't want to nuke it, just add a tablespoon of warm water to bring it up to body temperature.

Add a Meal Topper

We all like condiments on our food and cats are no exception. Sprinkle a cat-friendly, aromatic topping like [Dried Bonito Flakes](#).

Another tempting meal addition is [Virbac Rebound Recuperation Formula for Cats.](#) This is a palatable, easy-to-use formula rich in optimal vitamins and minerals, prebiotics, fatty acids and amino acids, designed to feed the gut and support recuperation in cats. Glutamine, Arginine, Taurine, Omega-3 & Omega-6 Fatty Acids and prebiotics to support gastrointestinal health and immune function, and support eating and drinking

Feed on Paper Plates

If your cat rejected food after you mixed medication into their meal, they can probably smell the residue in the bowl even after you washed it. Reduce the chance your cat will reject food by using paper plates at each serving, so they aren't reminded of the taste.

Consider an Appetite Stimulant

An appetite stimulant prescribed by your veterinarian can work wonders. If your cat won't eat, prescriptions can be written for medications including:

- Mirtazapine: This anti-depressant for humans that's been shown to have appetite-stimulant properties in cats.
- Another option is Cyproheptadine. It's an antihistamine also promotes eating. Ask your vet for a transdermal version that can be applied to the inner ear.
- Finally, a new option called Elura (Capromorelin Oral Solution) is now available and FDA-approved for cats.

Lack of appetite is common in any animal who's going through recovery, on pain medication or when fighting illness like cancer. Daily doses of pet medication can make inappetence worse. That's because medication often tastes terrible.

! TIP: Don't hide medication in your pet's normal meals if you want your cat to eat. If your pet has made it clear that certain medications are just unacceptable, you're going to need to get creative about giving them.

You're probably wondering "If I can't hide pills in food, how am I supposed to give medication to my Tripawd?" We've got that covered.

Disguise Medication with Store-Bought Pill Pastes, Wraps, Masks and Treats

If you're starting to get worried, reach for one of the many commercially-made pill pastes and wraps.

These products will keep your Tripawd from getting too used to the pill disguises you've already tried. The only issue with them is sometimes the ingredients aren't exactly health-conscious. Many include controversial fillers to get cats to eat them, including preservatives like BHT or corn syrup for flavoring. This is not ideal when you're aiming for a low-glycemic, anti-cancer diet for your Tripawd cat. On the other hand, as long these pill masks are given in small quantities, one can assume that the overall benefits of the medications are greater than the small risk these ingredients pose.

Sometimes you gotta do what you gotta do to get your cat to take pills. Just be conservative about using pill wraps and pastes.

! Always check ingredients for Xylitol when purchasing commercial products, as it can be harmful to pets!

Home Cooked Meals to Stimulate Appetite

Emily Parker of Catological.com shared several great tips to encourage your cat to eat, in the Tripawds Nutrition blog article: Help Your Tripawd Cat Recover with Home Cooked Meals.

> *Whether your cat has just come down with an illness or is recovering from surgery or a serious ailment such as cancer, it's vital they keep up their strength by eating. However, since cats are creatures of habit and like humans sometimes don't want to eat when they feel bad, you may have to get quite creative when figuring out what to feed them on their road to recovery.*
>
> – EMILY PARKER

Cook Up Ground Beef

Simple to prepare, all you need for a good serving is one-quarter pound of beef and some water. Once you've cooked the meat in a pan, put it in a blender and grind it up until it resembles canned food.

Tantalizing Turkey Meat Loaf

Turkey meat contains selenium, which is an important part of a cat's overall health. Try preparing a meat loaf made with turkey meat.

- 1/4 cup of boiled carrots
- 1/4 cup boiled peas
- 1/4 cup oats
- Two hard-boiled eggs and one raw egg

Heat your oven to 350 degrees.

Prepare the ingredients as you'd make a meat loaf for yourself.

Mix up everything in a bowl, transfer it to a loaf pan.

Bake it 45 minutes. Yum!

Whip Up Tasty Tuna Cake

For cats who are feeling ill, this can be one temptation that's almost too good to pass up.

- One can of tuna
- One egg
- 3 Tablespoons coconut flour
- 3 Tablespoons cottage cheese

Mix all ingredients together.

Pour the mixture into two cups of a muffin pan.

After baking for 20 minutes at 350 degrees, dinner is served!

When it's finished, you can even place a small amount of catnip on top, enticing kitty even more to take a bite. Hopefully these tricks will work to help you get your cat eating properly again after surgery. If not, you may need to resort to syringe feeding.

How to Feed Your Cat by Syringe

Syringe feeding a cat isn't as bad as it sounds. First, make a thin gruel with a bit of your cat's favorite canned food and some water.

- If possible, get a friend to help gently hold your cat in place.
- Have a paper towel ready, it makes an excellent bib.
- Allow your cat to express himself, don't panic.
- Use a 3cc syringe, the perfect size for a cat's mouth.
- Fill the syringe 1/4 of a milliliter at a time with the gruel.

- Come in from behind the cat's head. Don't touch the face and keep your fingers away from the mouth as much as possible.
- Place the tip of the syringe in a corner of the mouth. Slowly depress and allow your cat to eat.
- Feed a little at a time, don't force it and be patient.

More appetite stimulant ideas

Try these other great Tripawd-tested ideas to help stimulate your cat's appetite at feeding time

- Easy Fish and Meatballs Recipes for Cats and Dogs
- Pill Taking Treats, Strategies and Secret Recipes

Don't Overfeed! How and Why You Need to Keep the Pounds Off

After your Tripawd cat's appetite returns, you'll need to be extra vigilant about her weight. That's because any excess weight can put a three-legged cat at great risk for osteoarthritis and other obesity-related conditions.

For instance, did you know that a 15 pound cat is the equivalent of a woman who stands at just 5' 4" and weighs 218 pounds? Or a man who stands at 5' 9" and weighs 254 pounds? You may be shocked to find out what your cat would weigh if she were human. To find out, download the Pet-to-Human Weight Translators produced by the Association for Pet Obesity Prevention.

> *Every excess pound on an average DSH/DMH/DLH cat is equal to 14 to 15 pounds on a 5' 4" female or 17 pounds on a 5' 9" male.*
> - ASSOCIATION FOR PET OBESITY PREVENTION

! Weight management is critical for a healthy, injury-free life on three legs.

Tripawds can easily gain weight soon after surgery because of their decreased lack of stamina. And who can blame them: their bodies are compensating and using muscles in all new ways, leaving them sore and tired.

Many Tripawds lose enthusiasm over their usual exercise and playtime activities, which can lead to weight gain. Before you know it, your kitty has joined the growing pet obesity epidemic.

> *Hello everyone! New member here as well as new cat owner and I need some advice. I adopted Princess a week ago and she needs a bit of weight loss. She's 16 pounds and isn't very active, front leg amputee and is eating Science Diet Optimal Care dry food twice a day at the moment. I have a limited budget so I'd like to switch to a different food if possible. Thank you very much for any help!*
> – TWILEYFENNEC

Whether three legged or four, over 50 percent of domestic pets are overweight. It's why we share so many weight loss articles in the Tripawds Nutrition blog.

Even one extra pound can put serious stress on a Tripawd's remaining limbs and cause unnecessary mobility hardships. There is no more important role for you than to help your kitty keep the pounds off.

If you're unsure about your cat's optimal weight, the excellent article "Feline Obesity: An Epidemic of Fat Cats". This article by Dr. Lisa A. Pierson, DVM, is a great place to begin your research to help your cat stay slim.

> *Note that you should be able to easily feel the ribs with just a slight fat pad over them. Cats should also have a waist when viewed from above. They should not have any fat pads over their shoulders and if you pick up their skin, you should not feel thick fat underneath.*
> – IS YOUR CAT OVERWEIGHT?

Talk to your vet about weight management.

Looking for the best ways to help your Tripawd lose weight? Dr. Google only goes so far. You will achieve better success by working with your vet to pinpoint the right type and amount of food for your kitty.

Don't try to go it alone or your cat may fall ill to a condition like feline Hepatic Lipidosis (HL). This sometimes fatal fatty liver disease in cats occurs when a cat stops eating for more than two days or isn't getting enough calories over several days. As soon as your cat's stitches or staples are removed, ask your vet for a weight evaluation.

> *Weight loss in dogs and people is about 60 to 70 percent of what we eat, and only 30 to 40 percent what we burn."*
> – DR. ERNIE WARD, <u>WEIGHT LOSS IDEAS FOR PETS ON THREE (AND FOUR) LEGS</u>

When it comes to felines, "it's 90 percent diet and only 10 percent exercise," he explains. "That's because cats use glycogen for energy, which is a sugar, as opposed to dogs and humans (we use fatty acids as our primary energy source). So dogs and cats are completely different when it comes to their nutritional needs and calorie burns and all these things," he says. The trickier nature of feline physiology is why it's so important to work with your vet to help your cat lose weight.

"The most important decision that pet parents make every day regarding their pet's health is what they feed it," says Dr. Ward. "You've got the most powerful tool in your hand: the ability to precisely measure food every day."

❗ TIP: Learn Your Pet's Body Condition Score!

Similar to the Body Mass Index scale in people, the <u>Pet Body Condition Scoring Chart</u> is an easy way to gauge your Tripawd's weight. Your pet's weight check score will range from 1: Emaciated to 5: Obese. The BCS score determines the appropriate weight loss and exercise program for your Tripawd.

How to Know When Your Tripawd is at the Right Weight

In our article "<u>What is the Best Weight for a Tripawd Cat or Dog?</u>," Dr. Robin Downing explains how to know when your cat is at an ideal weight.

> *When my clients ask me, 'How will I know that we are there?/ I teach them about rib coverage. So, this is the participation part of the chat, so I have my clients take their hand and put their hand palm up and with the flats of their other fingers feel their knuckles and I say, 'Okay, with the flats of your fingers, that's too much rib coverage. Too much.*

Then I have them sit, Take that hand, put it palm down and make a fist and feel your knuckles. That's too little rib coverage.

Instead, it's a flat hand, palm down, feel your knuckles, that's perfect. We shouldn't see the ribs but we should be able to feel them easily right behind the shoulder blades." So, nice waist line at the end of the rib cage, tucked above them and that kind of thing.

– <u>VET PAIN EXPERT, DR. ROBIN DOWNING</u>

Stick to the Pet Weight Loss Program.

If your pet needs to slim down, your vet will recommend the food and quantities to do it. Stick to the diet and be patient, weight loss doesn't happen overnight. If you're not thrilled about the brand your vet wants you try, speak up. A good vet will happily recommend alternatives. And if for some reason they won't, find another vet who is in alignment with your nutrition philosophies.

❗ TIP: Ask other Tripawd cat parents about weight loss pet foods in our Eating Healthy Forum topic.

Get Smart About Pet Food

Pet food is a confusing, controversial and endless topic of debate. What one person feels is a great diet, another might think is junk. The truth is that we've seen some Tripawds members live to a ripe old age eating cheap processed food – even those with cancer! However, whether those animals were thriving on the food or merely surviving, we don't know. But what we do know is that one of the most important questions to ask yourself when you're trying to decide what to feed your cat is:

Would I put this on my plate for dinner?

If the answer is no, then shop for the best food you can afford.

Here's something else to consider: before you reach for a bag of kibble, you should know that more veterinarians with a strong interest in nutrition are recommending wet cat food over dry. Most bagged kibble is the equivalent of a diet of Doritos, soda, and cheeseburgers.

- Dry food lacks enough water content for optimal urinary tract health.
- It's loaded with carbs, which get stored as fat and cause obesity.
- And there isn't enough animal-based proteins for the needs of felines.

The protein levels in pet food is probably the most misunderstood aspect of the buying decision for us pet parents. If your cat has been diagnosed with cancer you may have heard that a high-protein, low carb diet is best. Since many pet foods now carry the grain-free label, it's easy to think that we are doing our pet a favor by switching to it. But before you commit to that new bag, understand that all proteins are not created equal.

Many grain-free pet foods contribute to the pet obesity problem.

That's because instead of corn and wheat fillers, manufacturers turn to high carbohydrate, fattening ingredients such as pea protein and potatoes. Scrutinize all grain free food before buying.

We aren't nutrition experts, so rather than get into a debate about what cat food brand is best or worst, let's focus on a few core ingredients that integrative medicine veterinarians say we should avoid.

Harmful Cat Food Ingredients to Avoid

From Holistic Veterinarian Dr. Karen Becker, DVM:

- **Powdered Cellulose**: Inhibits digestion and absorption of many vital nutrients
- **Dried Peas**: A poor substitute for animal protein and may contribute to GI disturbances
- **Alfalfa**: Another poor substitute for animal protein; contains plant estrogens that are well-documented endocrine disruptors, and interferes with absorption of essential nutrients.

Source: Keeps Your Pet From Absorbing Nutrients - And You Won't Believe How Trendy It Is

A Look at Questionable Ingredients, from integrative veterinarian Dr. Patrick Mahaney, DVM

- **Butylated Hydroxyanisole** (BHA) and **Butylated Hydroxytoluene** (BHT): A known carcinogen (cancer causing ingredient) banned in many countries for pets and people – except the U.S.
- **Ethoxyquin**: Illegal in human foods in the U.S. and harmful if it is swallowed or directly contacts skin.
- **Propylene Glycol** (PG): A chemical derivative of ethylene glycol (EG), also known as antifreeze, which is extremely toxic for any animal (or person) to consume.

Source: Pet Food Ingredients: The Bad

Want to learn more about cat food basics and what to look for in a brand? Check out the resources listed below.

Nutrition Insight for Cats with Cancer

Choosing the best food for a healthy cat is hard. Picking the right diet for cats with cancer is even tougher. As pet parents we want to do our best to help our cats have a fighting chance at winning the cancer battle, but unfortunately the internet is full of bad and conflicting information about what pets should and should not eat after being diagnosed. Even veterinarians can't always agree on the right foods to keep the disease under control.

You'll get different answers depending on who you ask. For example, if you asked Mercola's holistic veterinarian Dr. Karen Becker about carbs, she will tell you to avoid them.

> *Cancer cells need the glucose in carbohydrates to grow and proliferate. If you limit or eliminate that energy source, you do the same with the cancer's growth. That's one of the reasons I always discourage feeding diets high in carbohydrates. Carbs are pro-inflammatory nutrients that also feed cancer cells.*
> – CANCER AND YOUR PET: TWO THINGS TO AVOID

But if you mention carbs to any of the ACVN Board Certified Veterinary Nutritionists from the "Ask the Veterinary Nutritionist" panel at PetDiets.com, they say that eliminating carbs is an unscientific way to feed a pet with cancer:

> *The low carbohydrate diet for cancer is grossly over rated and without valid supportive data. The original research was done in Labradors with lymphoma and those that ate the high fat diet lived ~50 days longer. The design was problematic because the diets have many different features, not just fat to carb ratio. This study has never been repeated in the last 10 yrs although others have tried.*
>
> – PETDIETS.COM

A Middle Ground on Carbs and Cancer

There is at least one veterinary oncologist who takes a middle stance about carbs and pet cancer diets; Dr. Sue Ettinger, DVM, Dip. ACVIM (Oncology), co-author of The Dog Cancer Survival Guide. In this article she is discussing dogs, but the principles apply to cats too:

> *While there is little scientific data specifically showing feeding such a diet helps treat the dog cancer, as long as the diet is balanced, I think there is no harm, in my opinion.*
>
> *Remember: carbs are not all inherently bad, and some sources contain many valuable vitamins and minerals. Instead of generalizing "all carbs are bad," I think we should be more critical of the carbs source such as GMO (see above). For me, the grain-free diets are less important than the source of the grains. But I don't think you need to eliminate all carbs."*
>
> – DR. SUE ETTINGER, DIET AND DOGS WITH CANCER

Unfortunately there just aren't enough scientifically proven studies that point to the best diets for treating pet cancers. For now, most of the pet cancer nutrition information available is speculative and anecdotal. Success with any of them appears to be a hit-or-miss approach for vets and pet parents alike.

But we know you want to do something. Before you purchase tons of supplements that may be useless at best and cause drug interactions at worst, check out these additional tips to help your pet fight cancer with food.

Make sure your cat is eating.

If the only thing your cat will eat is cheap treats from the grocery store, then feed away. The last thing you want is for a cat with cancer to stop eating. Unfortunately this can be an uphill battle at times. Between the medications, supplements and any chemotherapy treatments, eating might be the last thing your cat wants to do. But only strong bodies can fight cancer, so keep your cat eating.

> *Remember that any food in the belly is more important then the best food sitting uneaten. Sometimes animals with cancer are so sick that they have very little appetite. In that case give them anything they will eat. When they are feeling better, focus on trying to get them to eat what is best for them.*
> – DR. LENA MCCULLOUGH, DVM,
>   DIETS FOR CANCER IN CATS AND DOGS

Feed Smaller Meals More Frequently

Dr. Korinn E. Saker, MS, DVM, PhD, Diplomate ACVN from the American College of Veterinary Nutrition suggests feeding in smaller quantities throughout the day.

Feeding Frequency - Providing the daily food allotment in smaller, frequent meals can be beneficial by:

▶ Enhancing overall nutrient uptake via the GI tract
▶ Minimizing intolerance due to meal volume
▶ Providing a sustained energy source throughout the day
▶ Decreasing stress associated with large meal feeding.

Change Up the Feeding Routine

If your pet gets picky and doesn't want to eat the meal plan you've prepared, try the strategies in this excellent white paper "Feeding a Pet During Chemotherapy" (originally shared by Bart the Tripawd Vizsla's Veterinary Nutritionist Dr. Susan G. Wynn, DVM, CVA, CVCH, AHG, the strategies are similar to how you fed your cat during amputation recovery.

Add Variety to Your Pet's Diet

If your pet refuses one food, offer a different one. Also try the following tactics to vary the stimulus properties of the food.

HOW TO HELP YOUR THREE LEGGED CAT

- Feed your cat from a different dish. Use a paper plate or a different bowl. Hand feeding or having your pet lick items off of a spoon might work as well.
- Feed your cat in a different room, away from people and other pets. This lack of distraction may help them to relax.
- Change the texture of your cat's food. Puree their food (even if it is already canned) to a very smooth texture… or go the opposite route and give textured foods or hard biscuits.
- Vary the temperature of your cat's food. Sometimes the smell of warm food will entice your pet. However, if your pet is nauseated, he may prefer cold food.
- Have someone else feed your cat. Oftentimes we are unaware of the nervous energy we project to our animals.

Fighting pet cancer is not an all-or-nothing choice. Even among holistic and conventional vets, theories about cancer nutrition for pets is always evolving. As you make your own choices about the best pet cancer diet for your Tripawd, below are two important things to remember if you want to help your pet live healthy.

Involve Your Veterinarian in Pet Nutrition Choices

Work with a veterinarian to find the best <u>Targeted Nutritional Therapy (TNT)</u> for your cat. Most vets did not receive advanced nutrition education while in vet school, but professional guidance is still an integral part of your pet's cancer battle. If your own vet isn't offering you the guidance you'd like, ask for a referral to a <u>board-certified veterinary nutritionist</u> who can educate you about things like daily caloric requirements for your cat, what medications may interfere with herbal supplements and tips for boosting your cat's appetite.

If you don't like what you hear from a veterinarian schooled in western approaches to cancer care, get a referral to a pet nutrition expert from the <u>American Holistic Veterinary Medical Association</u>.

Never forget that your cat is unique in every way.

What worked for one may not work for yours. It's OK to try

other plans you've read about, but if your cat doesn't like them, don't fret. Focus on what your pet likes to eat or you may be reducing their quality of life instead of enhancing it.

Pet Cancer Diet Nutrition Resources

The American Academy of Veterinary Nutrition lists the following pet cancer diet resources for pet parents who want to explore pet cancer diets with a veterinary nutritionist.

- Pet Nutrition Consulting: Nutritional consultations for veterinarians, pet owners and clients.
- Pet Diets.com: customized recipes for healthy pets, independent nutrition consultations for pets with medical conditions.
- Ohio State University Veterinary Medical Center Pet Nutrition Consulting: Request a pet nutrition consultation with OSU Nutrition Support Services.
- UC Davis Pet Nutrition Support Services provides nutritional consultations for vets whose clients wish to work with a board-certified nutritionist.

Post-Amputation Feline Fitness Tips

It wasn't too long ago when veterinarians assumed that once an animal was walking on three legs after surgery, they could go on doing whatever it was they did before the amputation. "She's good to go, let her go be a cat," they might say. But now we know better. Animals are living longer than ever and vets are noticing how a long-life on three legs can negatively impact the animal's body.

Here's what we know:

! A Tripawd is more prone to joint stress and osteoarthritis than their four-legged friends.

This is why it's crucial for new Tripawd pet parents to get smart about the best ways to exercise their cats. In this chapter we'll share a few general tips with you, then help you find a veterinary rehabilitation therapist to guide you and your Tripawd kitty toward better health and fitness for life.

Strong Core, Strong Tripawd

When it comes to cats you've probably never thought about how your kitty needs strong abdominals and core muscles. That's because just as humans need strong back and core muscles to avoid all types of injuries, it's even more important for three-legged pets.

In both dogs and cats, core muscle strength is critical for proper body alignment and maintaining balance during movement. Without it, a Tripawd is at a greater risk of spills and injury, just like a person.

All cats who participate in regular balance and core-strengthening workouts – like walking on uneven surfaces, sitting pretty, swatting at wand toys and playing on wobble boards – stand a better chance of living a long, healthy life.

For a Tripawd, it's especially important to participate in core strengthening and balance building activities on a regular basis. Tripawds of all ages are more susceptible to injury than four-leggers because every step places greater strain on their skeletal system. Their body is maneuvering it in ways that nature didn't intend for it to do.

For example, just as a human will compensate for an injury by limping on one leg, a three legged cat will adapt as an amputee with an altered gait and shorter, faster strides. Unfortunately this unnatural gait can eventually lead to upper or lower back pain and muscle strain, bone fractures and ligament tissue breakdown in both humans and canines.

Depending on your cat's pain threshold and pre-existing fitness level, these debilitating injuries usually appear so gradually that you don't notice until one day your cat lets her guard down and shows <u>classic pain indicators in cats</u>.

The good news is that pain doesn't have to be a part of your Tripawd's future if you get into a regular playtime routine of fun warm-ups, gentle exercise and stretching.

! Before you get started on any type of exercise program, please have your cat examined by your veterinarian (**preferably a certified animal rehabilitation expert**) to get a clean bill of health. When you start your Tripawd's new fitness program, remember to kick it off gradually and carefully to avoid injury. Watch closely for any signs of pain (refer to pain scale chart for indicators).

Dogs have enjoyed the benefits of rehab therapy exercises since the early 2000s. But cats have only recently started getting the attention they deserve in "physio" treatment. Most people don't even know that three-legged cat rehabilitation therapy exists – we sure didn't! We know better now, so the <u>Maggie Moo Fund for Tripawd Rehab</u> will reimburse anyone who takes their three legged cat (or dog) for evaluation by a certified animal rehab therapist.

Feta's Feline Rehabilitation Therapy Story

When Feta came along and applied for the <u>Tripawds Rehab Reimbursement Grant</u> we quickly discovered that not only is feline rehab therapy available, but it makes just a big difference in a Tripawd cat's life as it does in a dog's. Here's a short summary of Feta's story as shared in a <u>Tripawds News blog spotlight</u>.

"In summer 2016, Feta was found by Jersey City Animal Control along the side of the road, sickly, injured, presumably having been hit by a car, with a badly broken leg and a litter of nursing kittens at her side," her foster mom Cheesecat told us.

As she appeared to be very friendly, and therefore potentially adoptable, the decision was made to go ahead and try to save her, even though it would be an expensive undertaking.

The broken leg was amputated, but it got infected. She eventually healed but her strength did not return. Her foster mom took advantage of the <u>Maggie Moo Fund for Tripawd Rehab</u> so a professional could help Feta get strong and become adoptable.

Based on this experience, Feta's foster mom shared many helpful tips for three-legged cats, like in her blog post, <u>Feta's Claw Conundrums</u>.

> *To keep her entertained and working at least a little bit while on "medical leave," I picked up a couple of <u>puzzle toys</u> for her to force her to work for her food (even if she wasn't using that leg). Here you can see her using it, with the "help" of one of my foster kittens!*
> – CHEESECAT

Feta's people found Dr. Fellen and rehab nursing manager Jenn Stoller at the Westfield Veterinary Group in Westfield, NJ.

Dr. Stoller prescribed a combination of stretching and exercising Feta's bad leg in order to loosen and relax the muscles.

She also showed Feta's people how to help her practice weight bearing to strengthen the leg. Read more details about tri-kitty Feta's therapy experience in her Tripawds Foundation rehab article and Feta's tri-kitty blog.

> *Despite all of this unpleasantness, Feta Cat remains truly delightful, kind, and gentle. All in all, I think she is enjoying life, even if I make her do ouchy exercises and switched her to the "fat cat" kibble!*
> – FETA'S MOM

Tripawd Cats Enjoy the Benefits of Rehab Therapy.

Another recipient of the Tripawds Foundation Rehab Reimbursement Grant, Saysha survived a dog attack and bounced back relatively well. But her human knew she would be better off with additional post-op rehab care. Saysha's human Vanessa reported the following after her first rehab visit.

Saysha's doctor prescribed:
- laser therapy twice a week to help with pain management
- metabolizing dry food diet to help her lose two pounds
- a warm compress on her back and shoulder after long sleeps to help with stiffness and pain
- massage of the lumbar region, neck and all over to relax muscles
- two supplements (Duralactin and Free Form) which help with inflammation and overall health

She is also doing four daily exercises which include:
- passive or active joint extension x10 for the shoulder and elbow
- full extension stretches enabled by pointing a laser part way up a wall 1 to 2x daily for two minutes,
- feather on a stick play once a day or every other day for 1-2 minutes at a time
- low wheelbarrowing which involves lifting her from the abdomen and slowing moving her forward for 30 seconds once a day

Anyone can do these exercises with their new Tripawd kitty, but having a professional guide you thorough the process is beneficial for you as well as your cat. Vanessa reports that "**The thing I have learned above all is how well cats can hide their pain.** I was also ignorant to the fact that her kangaroo style of walking was a sign that she was not doing as well as I thought."

How to Find a Rehab Therapy Practitioner

Awareness of the benefits of animal rehabilitation therapy is growing. But this aspect of post-op care is often left out of conversations between vets and clients. Animal rehabilitation is still a new field in veterinary medicine. Sometimes it's referred to as "physical therapy" in the States, or "physiotherapy" in Europe. Most vet professionals prefer that you call it "rehabilitation therapy" since many state laws say that the term "physical therapy" can only be used when referring to human care.

Regardless, it's a safe bet to say that most family vets do not have training in animal rehabilitation therapy or possess a comprehensive understanding of its benefits. When a cat loses a leg, nearly all family vets tell clients to continue life as normal after the Tripawd patient recovers from surgery. We wish they wouldn't.

Why Cats Benefit from Rehab Therapy

Just ask any animal rehabilitation practitioner how a new amputee should prepare for life on three legs and the suggestions will usually differ from what family vets say. A rehab practitioner will tell you that even if you choose to do nothing else, at least have your cat evaluated so you can learn how to watch for potential problems. You can practice injury prevention and learn how to lead rehab games at home on your own.

Animal rehab practitioners can help your Tripawd in many ways, including:
- Locating existing skeletal and muscular weaknesses to reduce the risk of additional damage.
- Diagnosing and fixing a physical problem instead of relying solely on painkillers to hide symptoms.
- Correcting your Tripawd's gait to reduce the physical stress of the "Tripawd Hop"
- Preventing trauma by strengthening core abdominal muscles required for balance and stamina.

- Helping you gain confidence as you watch your Tripawd get stronger.
- Entertaining and challenging your cat, physically and mentally.
- Improving the overall quality of life for both of you.

Considerations for Choosing a Practice for Rehabilitation Services

Don't be surprised if your vet hasn't heard about animal rehabilitation therapy. Too many still assume that Tripawds can just go on with life without additional specialized care. But if you find a practitioner who understands the value of rehab therapy, you'll decrease the risk of injury, osteoarthritis and other painful conditions in your amputee cat.

Veterinary Rehabilitation Certifications:
- **CCRT:** Certified Canine Rehabilitation Therapist
- **CCRP:** Certified Canine Rehabilitation Practitioner
- **AARV:** American Association of Rehabilitation Veterinarians Certification
- **VMRT:** Veterinary Massage and Rehab Therapy Program Credential

! NOTE: There is no current certification for feline rehab therapists, but most practitioners with these credentials are qualified to offer rehabilitation treatment for cats.

Tips to Find the Most Qualified Rehab Therapist

Step 1: Get a referral from your vet.

Let your vet know that you are interested in finding a licensed rehab therapist for your cat. If they don't have a referral, move on to Step 2.

Step 2: Find a clinic with rehabilitation staff who carry "AARV" "CCRT" or "CCRP" credentials.

Working with a credentialed practitioner is key to a safe and helpful experience. At this time, there are no official feline specific certifications, but rest assured that anyone with these letters after their name are the most highly trained people in animal rehabilitation therapy. These letters mean they have graduated from one of the accredited formal courses recognized for outstanding training and education of veterinarians, vet techs and vet nurses.

- The Canine Rehabilitation Institute which awards the certificate of Canine Rehabilitation Therapist (CCRT)
- The University of Tennessee's Outreach and Continuing Education Department, which awards the Certified Canine Rehabilitation Practitioner (CCRP) certificate.
- The American Association of Rehabilitation Veterinarians (AARV) offers various veterinary rehab credential programs (CCRT, CCRP, CERP, and VMRT).
- In Canada, The Animal Rehabilitation Division (ARD) offers a Diploma in Canine Rehab exclusively to human physiotherapists.
- In the UK: Find a physio therapist from The Institute of Registered Veterinary and Animal Physiotherapists.
- In Australia: Find certified practitioners in the Australian Canine Rehabilitation Association Directory.

When you reach out to these practitioners, let them know you are looking for someone who can help you with your cat. If they don't offer feline rehab, ask if they know another practitioner who does. It may take some doing but eventually you may find a practice near you.

Another good resource is your nearest veterinary teaching hospital that has a sports medicine department. The Tripawds News blog article "How to Get Affordable, Awesome Veterinary Care for Your Tripawd" details the benefits of working with a vet school.

Get Free Rehab for Your Tri-kitty

The benefits of seeing a qualified veterinary rehabilitation specialist are endless, but we also realize that not everyone has the ability to pay for one. That's why the Tripawds Foundation will reimburse members up to $200 for a first time visit to a certified rehab practitioner for an initial consultation! For details, read:

- Get Your Tripawd Fit, On Us!
  https://tripawds.org/2015/09/vet-rehab-reimbursement/

What to Expect from Veterinary Rehabilitation Therapy

As pet parents we get just as much from a visit with a veterinary rehab therapist than our cats!

For instance, a good clinic will provide you with:
- An evaluation of your Tripawd cat to look for areas that need improvement.
- An understanding of where your Tripawd might be experiencing pain, and how to alleviate it.
- New games, activities and other fun things you can do at home to help your Tripawd get strong and stay there
- Nutrition counseling to help your cat stay slim.
- A point of contact who can serve as a fast resource when, not if, your Tripawd develops chronic pain issues.

Animal rehab therapy clinics aren't on every corner yet, but the service is growing fast in response to pet parents asking for it. Feline rehab therapists can be tricky to locate, but more are starting practices every day. Practitioners are adapting the therapies devised for dogs and turned them into suitable programs for cats. Everything from passive range of motion to massage to <u>acupuncture</u> to water therapy can be adapted for feline rehab therapy.

> *We have to talk to cats differently, train them differently when using these techniques, but they are capable of doing what dogs do in the world of rehab.*
> - <u>DR. ROBIN DOWNING</u>, PET PAIN EXPERT

! TIP: In the Cornell CatWatch article, "<u>Feline Physical Rehabilitation</u>," you can learn what therapy techniques and modalities reduce pain and promote healing.

When you're trying to locate a clinic, <u>Dr. Amy Kramer</u>, PT, DPT, CCRT, therapy director at Beach Animal Rehabilitation Center in Los Angeles recommends practices that have a veterinarian and a licensed rehabilitation practitioner working together.

"If there's no therapist and no veterinarian involved, then I think you're missing a link in the chain of what works," she says. This collaborative approach works because rehabilitation veterinarians are trained to recognize and diagnose animal diseases, but animal rehab practitioners are not.

When an animal is undergoing rehab therapy but her condition is not being monitored by a rehabilitation veterinarian, small signs of disease and illness could be missed, which puts the patient's health in jeopardy and possibly lead to additional treatment costs.

DIY Therapy Exercises for Cats

Whether human or animal, we all need strong core muscles (abdominals) to keep us from injuring our backs and hips during movement. Much has been written about core strengthening exercises for dogs, but not as much for cats. Thanks to the Tripawds community, we are all learning about practical and fun ways to help cats get strong. **We hear it all the time: "But I Can't Find a Therapist Near Me."**

If you cannot locate a feline rehab therapist close enough to you, don't give up. The 2020 pandemic kick started online pet rehabilitation consulting all over the globe! Call the toll-free Tripawds Helpline and we may be able to help find a qualified clinic near you.

There are also things you can do at home to help your cat get and stay strong. But before you attempt any of these DIY feline rehab therapy exercises, please check with your vet to make sure these activities are safe for your cat.

Start with Massage Therapy

Massage improves circulation, speeds healing, increases flexibility, relieves stress, aids socialization, relaxes the body, enhances the human/animal bond, and feels great! In the PetPlace.com article How to Massage Your Cat, we discovered that the following basic principles outlined in our How to Massage Your Tripawd article also apply to cats.

▶ Effleurage is the first thing you will do when beginning a massage. This is a hand-over-hand technique where you are running your hands over your pet's body, from head to tail.

▶ Gentle rocking motions are comforting, and warms up the body, keeping the muscles loose and less prone to injury. This technique will also help strengthen the muscles.

Your goal is to avoid any infection sites, bony areas, open wounds and lumps. Read the entire article for <u>more instructions about massaging your cat</u>.

You might also want to check out the <u>PawWave Massager</u> tool. It provides gentle vibration therapy to relieve muscle tension around delicate tissue or sore spots. This version is ideal for new Tripawd amputation pain. It can increase lymphatic drainage & decrease swelling after exertion, injury or surgery.

Fun and Easy Workout Games for Cats

Working out doesn't have to be complicated or expensive. <u>Purrkins works hard</u> to stay in great shape using simple equipment, some home-made, some store bought.

One simple exercise to help develop core strength is stretching on an unstable surface. Encourage your cat to reach up from a sitting position on an unstable surface. Couch cushions can be used, or you can purchase a <u>Balance Pad</u>. Using a <u>Balance Disc</u> provides a greater challenge which you can be adjusted with inflation.

Another rehab fan is <u>tri-kitty Smore</u>, who enjoys working her core muscles using ordinary cat toys.

> *She has mastered the meerkat pose as well where she balances on her hind legs. In fact, she's easily able to sit up and grab toys on wand toys and stuff them in her mouth with her front paw.*
> – SMORE

Mona also enjoyed stretching fun.

> *The chiro vet said it's also important to keep a good range of motion in the front leg so one good way is to have the cat reach forward – like for a feather or food bowl. I hold the bowl high up so she does a good stretch with her front leg.*
> – MONA

Two More Fun Ways to Exercise a Three-Legged Cat

The word "cats" and "exercise" don't seem to go together, do they? Well, according to one rehab vet, they do! Start by using food as a training tool, suggests Dr. Amber Callaway Lewis, founder of Treasure Coast Animal Rehabilitation in Vero Beach, Florida.. One way or another, food gets most felines motivated enough to burn extra calories.

Fun with Cat Kibble, Part 1

Kick start any exercise session by dividing up one cup of cat kibble into a few small bowls. Then place them all around the house. "There's no reason your cat who sleeps all day can't walk to get their food!" says Dr. Lewis. In our article, "Two Fun Tripawd Cat Exercise Tips Anyone Can Do!" she reviews these exercises and more.

Great places to put your kitty's food include a low step, or on the couch so your Tripawd cat has to actively step or reach up to get it. Whatever you do, don't hide your cat's food. That's not motivating at all! Make sure your cat sees where you place the goodies, so she knows where to reach for them.

Fun with Cat Kibble, Part 2

Next, Dr. Lewis suggests putting your Tripawd cat's normal amount of kibble into your pocket. Consider this simple way to make her work for her food.

Then, drop one kibble at a time while making sure your cat sees you do it. Walk all over your home, dropping a little kibble here and a little kibble there. This should motivate your three-legged cat to walk around and burn calories.

Remember to Add Traction

These Tripawd cat exercise tips are great, but they work even better if your home has lots of traction for your kitty. Always make sure your cat has safe, slip-proof places to walk. Get carpet runners or bulk yoga mats and place them in areas that make it easy for your amputee cat to go from one room to another. "Once they know they're secure on three legs," says Dr. Lewis, "you can just grow together from there."

Thank You!

We are so happy you decided to read this book. And thank you for advocating for your Tripawd's long term health and happiness. Based on our own experiences and input from Tripawds community members, we believe this book covers all of the basics about a cat's life on three legs. If you believe there is something we have left out, or anything we should address in more detail, let us know.

Want to share details about your Tripawd kitty's experience? Please do! The more information we can share, the more we all learn from each other. Consider starting a Tripawds Blog or visit the Tripawds Discussion Forums to share your story.

Let's keep working together to expand our knowledge and show the world that, **It's better to hop on three legs than to limp on four!**

- Rene Agredano and Jim Nelson
  Founders, Tripawds – tripawds.com
  Authors, Be More Dog – bemoredog.net

- With generous assistance from Holly, mom to Purrkins
  – purrkins.tripawds.com

Team #Tripawds with Wyatt Ray at the 2018 Western Veterinary Conference

Appendix

What is Tripawds?

Tripawds.com is a user-supported online community for animal amputees and their people maintained by Jim Nelson (aka: Admin) and René Agredano (aka: Jerry). The site offers free blogs for those facing a cancer diagnosis and/or amputation for their cat or dog, as well as a place to share their experiences, treatment plans and results, and offer support to others.

Launched in 2006, the Tripawds Community is the primary resource for researching the real world experiences of other three legged pets – featuring the popular discussion forums, live chat room and more than 2,000 member blogs.

The Tripawds Foundation

Founded in 2014, the Tripawds Foundation is a 501c3 charity established to help facilitate our many free community resources and direct assistance programs. We maintain the growing list of Tripawds Foundation programs to assist anyone facing decisions about amputation for their cats and dogs. See if you qualify for assistance or support the cause to help Tripawds everywhere with veterinary financial aid, free gear, and much more.

Tripawds Assistance Programs

- Maintaining the public benefit Tripawds Community
- Free vet patient outreach materials
- Hosting the Toll-free Tripawds Helpline
- The Tripawds Rescue Fund
- Reimbursement for certified rehab consultations
- Amputation Surgery Assistance Program
- Tripawds Gear Fund
- And more with your support!

Free Tripawds Community Resources

Tripawds Discussion Forums (tripawds.com/forums) Members are waiting to hear your story and offer support. Search topics for answers to common questions in our Three Legged Cats Forum. Registered members can use the Private Messaging system to communicate directly, and privately, with others.

Tripawds Live Chat (tripawds.com/chat) Feeling stressed? Need someone to talk to? Chat live with members who understand what you're going through. Log-in is required. tripawds.com/chat

Jerry's Tripawds News Blog (tripawds.com/progress) The primary news source for three legged pets and their people.

The Tripawds Gear Shop (gear.tripawds.com) Shop the Tripawds Gear Shop for Reviews, recommendations and demo videos for the best harnesses, life vests and other products to help three legged pets.

The Tripawds Nutrition blog (nutrition.tripawds.com) Diet, supplements, medications, oh my! Get the best food and supplement recommendations plus interviews with veterinary nutrition experts.

The **Tripawds Photo Galleries** (tripawds.com/gallery) and **Video Playlists** (tripawds.com/videos) featuring amazing examples of three legged pets, treatment and recovery, and life on three legs.

Tripawds Blogs Directory (tripawds.com/blogs) Tripawds hosts free three legged pet blogs for anyone who wishes to share their cat's story or document their chosen treatment plan. Tripawds Supporter Blogs with enhanced features are available for a nominal fee. The following Featured Blogs focus on compiling specific information and resources relative to the care and treatment of pet cancer survivors and other amputee animals.

▶ See all 100+ tri-kitty blogs here. (https://tri.pet/trikitties)

Tripawds News Newsletter (tripawds.com/subscribe) Subscribe to stay informed of important updates, informative blog posts, and popular forum posts, as well as greatest hits from more than ten years of Tripawds News.

Tripawd Talk Radio (tripawds.com/radio) Hosted by Tripawds founders Rene Agredano and Jim Nelson, subscribe on your favorite podcast app for informative discussions with veterinary surgeons, oncologists, rehab therapists and other specialist veterinarians.

And much more!

We started Jerry's blog upon receiving his cancer diagnosis in November, 2006 to share his progress with family and friends. Since adding discussion forums, membership has grown to more than 20,000 registered users. For complete details about why and how we turned Tripawds into our full-time labor of love, read our book ***Be More Dog: Learning to Live in the Now***.

Our Goal at Tripawds: To help three legged pets and their people everywhere.

The Tripawds Foundation Mission Statement:

> *To maintain a community of support for those faced with amputation for their cats and dogs, by providing informational resources and a platform for discussion.*

The Tri-kitty Required Reading List

Consider these articles and books we have reviewed for help coping with your cat's amputation, recovery and treatment.

What to Expect?

Browse our ongoing series of **"What to Expect" Articles About Amputation**, for everything from preparing for amputation surgery to life on three legs in and outside the home.

Amputation Surgery and Recovery

- [Tips for Three-legged Cats During and After Amputation Recovery](https://tripawds.com/2016/11/02/tips-for-three-legged-cats/)
  https://tripawds.com/2016/11/02/tips-for-three-legged-cats/
- [Cat Amputation Recovery Shopping List](https://gear.tripawds.com/2021/11/18/cat-amputation-recovery-shopping-list/)
  https://gear.tripawds.com/2021/11/18/cat-amputation-recovery-shopping-list/
- [Litterbox Tips for New Tripawd Cats](http://tripawds.com/2016/06/15/litterbox-tips-tripawd-cats/)
  http://tripawds.com/2016/06/15/litterbox-tips-tripawd-cats/
- [How Pheromone Anti-Anxiety Therapy Helps New Tripawd Cats, Dogs](http://amazon.tripawds.com/2016/01/21/feliway-amputation-cats-dogs/)
  http://amazon.tripawds.com/2016/01/21/feliway-amputation-cats-dogs/

Pain Management

- Best (and Worst) Pet Amputation Pain Drugs
  https://tripawds.com/2020/09/16/pet-amputation-pain-drugs/
- Learn to Recognize Pain Signs in Cats
  https://tripawds.com/2022/01/12/tripawd-cat-pain/
- All About Gabapentin for Tripawds
  https://tripawds.com/2019/09/11/how-gabapentin-works-in-tripawds/
- Is Your Vet Following Current Pain Management Guidelines?
  https://tripawds.com/2022/04/06/aaha-pet-pain-management-guidelines/
- Heat and Ice Therapy Tips
  https://gear.tripawds.com/2021/09/30/warm-compress-and-cold-packs/

Feline Cancer

- Vaccine Associated Sarcoma Cats Share Stories and Information
  https://tripawds.com/forums/3-legged-cats/vaccine-associated-sarcoma-fibrosarcoma-osteosarcoma-chondrosarcoma/
- Cat Cancer, Oncology and Radiation Realities
  http://tripawds.com/2017/09/06/cat-cancer-oncology
- More About Cat Cancer, Oncology and Radiation Therapy
  http://tripawds.com/2017/09/13/cat-cancer-oncology-and-radiation/

Eating Healthy

- The Easy Way to Syringe Feed Tripawd Cats
  http://nutrition.tripawds.com/2017/11/06/syringe-feed-tripawd-cats/
- Amputation Recovery Supplement Helps Tripawds Get Healthy
  http://nutrition.tripawds.com/2016/10/24/amputation-recovery-supplement/
- Help Tripawd Cats Recover With Home Cooked Meals
  http://nutrition.tripawds.com/2018/01/04/tripawd-cat-recover/

APPENDIX

- Easy Fish and Meatballs Recipes for Cats and Dogs
  http://nutrition.tripawds.com/2017/07/31/meatballs-recipes-for-cats-and-dogs/
- Easy Grain-Free Salmon Treats Recipe
  http://nutrition.tripawds.com/2016/06/02/grain-free-salmon-tripawd-treats-recipe/
- Do Cats Need Joint Supplements?
  https://nutrition.tripawds.com/2015/03/16/cat-joint-supplements/
- Pet-to-Human Weight Translators – a Tripawd Reality Check
  http://nutrition.tripawds.com/2018/04/02/pet-to-human-weight-translators/

Hopping Around

- The Best Harness for Three-Legged Cats is Here!
  https://gear.tripawds.com/2017/04/27/the-best-harness-for-three-legged-cats-is-here/
- The Suitical Pet Recovery Suit Makes Amputation Healing a Snap!
  https://gear.tripawds.com/2018/01/25/suitical-pet-recovery-suit/
- Easy DIY Pet Surgery Recovery Suit for Cats and Dogs
  https://gear.tripawds.com/2016/11/17/diy-pet-surgery-recovery-suit/
- DIY Tripawd Cat Traction Socks for Slippery Floors
  http://gear.tripawds.com/2015/09/30/tripawd-cat-traction-socks/
- Food Puzzles for Cats Make Great Tripawd Therapy
  http://amazon.tripawds.com/2016/12/08/food-puzzles-for-cats/
- DIY Core Strengthening Exercises for Cats
  https://downloads.tripawds.com/2017/01/09/diy-core-strengthening-exercises-for-cats/
- Tri-kitty Maceo's Cat Cancer Supplements, Tips and Ideas
  https://nutrition.tripawds.com/2017/11/13/cat-cancer-supplements/

Tri-kitty Parent Experiences

- Tripawd Cats Share Tails About Amputation, Life on Three Legs (Tripawd Talk Radio episode #36)

http://downloads.tripawds.com/2014/08/25/tripawd-cats-share-tails-about-amputation-life-on-three-legs/
- Let's Talk Tripawd Cats, Dogs and Rehab Therapy with Dr. Kennedy (Tripawd Talk Radio episode #42)
http://tripawds.com/2014/11/05/lets-talk-tripawd-cats-dogs-and-rehab-therapy-with-dr-kennedy/
- Sebastian Shares His Best Tips for Tripawd Cats
http://tripawds.com/2015/10/28/amputee-cat-tips/
- Learn All About Three Legged Cats at #WVC2017
http://tripawds.com/2017/03/08/about-three-legged-cats/
- Purrkins' Lessons for Tripawd Kitties
http://tripawds.com/2016/11/22/tripawd-tuesday-purrkins-lessons-for-tripawd-kitties/
- Ten Things To Know About Tripawd Cats
http://tripawds.com/2016/08/03/three-legged-cats-video/
- Tripawd Kitty Bloggers Share Their Feline Amputation Tales
http://tripawds.com/2014/04/21/trikitties/
Start your free blog in minutes!
https://tripawds.com/blogs

Bonus Materials

The following pages include helpful worksheets, charts, and checklists you can print to help you help your cat make the most of life on three legs:

- Daily Regimen / Caregiver Information
- Exercise Routine Worksheet
- Weekly Diet and Nutrition Worksheet
- Important Veterinary Questions
- Feline Body Conditioning Scoring Chart
- Feline Acute Pain Scale Chart

! This section is available in the Premium e-book. Get $5 OFF with Coupon Code BASIC5.
https://tri.pet/tricatbook

Acknowledgments

Cool Tips for Tripawd Cats is the third in our series of e-books based on informative content compiled from years of interviews with veterinary professionals and the shared experiences, tips and suggestions of pet parents from around the world who participate in the Tripawds Blogs community.

Like the Tripawds website, this book is intended to be an interactive research tool. The ideas we share represent the personal experiences of members who have learned how to make the most of life on three legs in a variety of circumstances.

None of the information contained on Tripawds or found within these pages is meant to replace one-on-one medical care from your regular veterinary team.

We dedicate this book to every Tripawds member, including **YOU!** From submitting guest blog posts and <u>charitable contributions</u> to taking time from your busy day to participate in the forums, Tripawds would not be able to help others through their own three-legged journey without the inspawrational stories of people like yourself. there are many ways to <u>share your story!</u>

In addition, we would like to express our sincere gratitude to every veterinary professional who's kindly helped us provide accurate and current information to the Tripawds community.

Thank you from the bottom of our hearts. Without your participation and <u>generous support</u>, Tripawds would not be such the very special place that it is has become.

With gratitude,

▶ **René Agredano and Jim Nelson**
With Tripawd Angels Jerry & Wyatt Ray

Tripawds Publications

Three Legs and a Spare

Loving Life on Three Legs

Cool Tips for Tripawd Cats

Be More Dog: Learning to Live in the Now

Tripawd Heroes

The KillBarney Tour

Find All Tripawds E-books at:
https://downloads.tripawds.com

Tripawds Foundation

Find information about assistance programs and how you can help at:

https://tripawds.org

ALSO FROM TRIPAWDS FOUNDERS
RENE AGREDANO & JIM NELSON:

Be More Dog: Learning to Live in the Now

Enjoying Every Day to the Fullest on the Road to Happiness

"I love that they got in the RV and did it for their dog, Jerry."
– OPRAH WINFREY (THE GAYLE KING SHOW, MAY 2010)

Be More Dog is the inspiring story of how one dog with terminal cancer led his people on a spiritual journey that turned their life around and opened their eyes to the importance of living in the Now.

When their heart and soul dog Jerry lost a leg to cancer, Jim Nelson and Rene Agredano sold their home, their business, and nearly everything they owned to enjoy their final days traveling together as a pack in a new RV. Given just months to live, Jerry led his people around the country for two years.

Be More Dog is more than a memoir about a three-legged dog on an epic road trip. It is a mantra to live by, and this book is the guide.

This heartwarming tale is filled with deep meaning. Through his actions and attitude in the face of adversity, Jerry shows Jim and Rene how important it is to live in the now—to persevere when the going gets tough, to never give up, and that every day is a great day, no matter what life throws your way.

#1 New Release in Travel with Pets
#1 New Release in Veterinary Surgery

With foreword by MUTTS creator Patrick McDonnell!

Available everywhere books are sold.
Find special gift edition and bonus material at:
https://bemoredog.net

Made in the USA
Columbia, SC
13 July 2024